OVERSEAS INDIANS

Extracts from reviews of
Fiji: A Precarious Coalition
Shubha Singh

"Shubha Singh's knowledge of Fiji's history and politics is both deep and extensive.... The book is most timely and worth reading." —**K Natwar Singh**, *Frontline*

"She writes with empathy for both Fijian Fijians and Fijian Indians. A book for anyone who wishes to inform himself of the story of a happy land caught in the middle of avoidable ethnic crisis." —**Aravinda R Deo**, *India Today*

"Singh takes the unusual route of explaining the conflict in Fiji through the experience of her own family.... Singh's book is essential reading in understanding the complexities that led to the turmoil and why the Fijians balked at the idea of having a prime minister who was ethnically Indian."
—**Bhaichand Patel**, *Outlook*

"The study (of Fiji) is outstanding and topical and is of interest to anybody in understanding Indian diaspora."
— **Ganganath Jha**, *The Book Review*

OVERSEAS INDIANS
The Global Family

SHUBHA SINGH

Maulana Abul Kalam Azad Institute of Asian Studies, Kolkata

SHIPRA

ISBN: 81-7541-225-9

First Published in India in 2005

Overseas Indian: The Global Family

Published by:
SHIPRA PUBLICATIONS
115-A, Vikas Marg, Shakarpur
Delhi-110092, INDIA
Phone: 91-11-55277210, 91-11-22500954
Fax: 91-11-22458662
E-mail: info@shiprapublications.com
www.shiprapublications.com

Laser Typesetting by:
Sunshine Graphics
Delhi-110032

Printed at:
Choudhary Offset Process
Delhi-110051

Preface

My family has been linked to the Indian diaspora ever since my great grandparents, Ramchander and Padam Kaur travelled to Fiji Islands as indentured workers in 1885. My great grandparents returned home to their village in Agra district with their Fiji born son, Bere Singh after 16 years. My grandfather, Bere Singh also went to Fiji to work and on retiring from his job in the colonial administration returned to Jaingara village. In 1971 when Fiji gained its independence my father, Bhagwan Singh was appointed India's High Commissioner to Fiji. The family's connection with Fiji acquired another strand when my brother, Ajay Singh married Shiromani Maharaj, whose family is one of the prominent business families of Suva. Shiromani's brothers and sister live in Fiji, Australia and New Zealand.

In 1965, changes in the American immigration regulations opened migration for persons with occupational skills required in the United States. My brother-in-law, Karan Pal Singh was among the Indian engineers and doctors who went to America shortly thereafter. In 1967, my sister, Abha married Karan Pal Singh and went out to live in Michigan where their two sons, Samir and Suneil were born. Samir was re-elected to city council in East Lansing, the capital of Michigan State for a second term two years ago.

I lived and worked in Fiji for four and a half years during a period of euphoria, when the newly independent island nation was hailed as a shining example of multi-racial harmony in the Pacific region. In May 2000, the government of Mahendra Chaudhry, Fiji's first Prime Minister of Indian origin was overthrown in an armed coup. In my book, *Fiji: A Precarious Coalition*, I drew from family history to write an account of the Indian experience in Fiji. I sought to analyse how and why the promise of the first decade and a half of racial amity deteriorated into armed overthrow of two elected governments seen to be dominated by Indians within a span of 13 years.

The experience of life in Fiji sparked off an interest in the larger diaspora. During my travels as a journalist I met people of Indian origin settled in a far flung countries, some in large diasporic communities and others in smaller groups. They included almost all sections of overseas Indians, from third and fourth generation descendants of Indian origin in Mauritius, Trinidad and South Africa to later day migrants to the developed countries. I saw the efforts at assimilation in these countries and also the craving to retain the cultural and spiritual ties with the motherland.

As the overseas community has grown into a vibrant, successful diaspora and modern day travel and communications have helped develop a closer connectivity with India, the Indian government has made concerted efforts to reach out to the diaspora. It is through my personal and historical experience of life of the overseas Indians that I have tried to analyse the manifold sections of the diaspora and their experiences in their adopted lands, the similarities and differences of their lives and their needs and perceptions. My reason for writing this book is to present the various processes which Indian communities went through in different regions of the world as they settled in new lands and adjusted to their new circumstances. It is those experiences that helped retain or modify their identities as ethnic Indians and give rise to their hopes and expectations from the ancestral homeland.

Shubha Singh

Contents

Chapter 1

Indians Abroad

Through the ages people have travelled afar to find land, food and work. Migration is an inseparable part of history and has been one of the abiding travel sagas of all times. The myth of Indians as a traditionally land-locked people does not reflect the reality of the sea faring coastal regions of India, which have had a tradition of high mobility and a long maritime history. Despite the taboo of crossing the black waters of the oceans for high caste Hindus, Indians were not afraid of the deep seas; they travelled far and wide through the centuries to visit new lands. They went to distant places as pilgrims, monks, artisans and teachers. There was thriving trade across the Indian Ocean through the centuries, and the signs of Indian settlements are still to be seen in Zanzibar, Ethiopia and along the African coast. One of the busiest maritime routes was from India through the Southeast Asian countries and on to coastal China. Towards the west was the trade route stretching across to the Persian Gulf and then on to the eastern coast of Africa.

Monks, traders and wayfarers took Buddhism through Central Asia to China, from Tibet to Mongolia and to Japan. Some lingering strands of India's connections with far-flung regions are still in existence. Certain Hindu customs remain a part of life in Thailand, Sanskrit names are still in use in Java and a version of the *Ramayana* legend survives in Indonesia. Hinduism spread through the Southeast Asian region and a number of Hindu kingdoms existed in the Indo-China region until the mid-thirteenth Century. India's ties with Malaya date back to antiquity, and the Tamil presence in Indonesia pre-dated the arrival of the Dutch colonisers. But the major Indian migration to these parts took place in the later half of the 19th Century when the need for plantation labour arose.

The great waves of Asian migration began when Europe's imperial powers established colonies in the New World to meet the demand for tropical commodities like rubber, sugarcane, tea and coffee in Europe. The colonies initial need for labour at the plantations, the tin and gold mines was met through slaves. But when slavery was abolished throughout the British Empire in 1833, the plantation owners urgently needed replacements for the African slave labour. A substitute work force was found in Indian and Chinese emigrant workers. There are estimates that over one and a half million Indians went overseas to earn a living in the 19th and early part of 20th century — to Burma, Malaya, Africa, the Caribbean and the Pacific islands.

In 1938 T. S. Rajagopal described the overseas Indians as "spread over a belt which runs around the Equator from the North Atlantic over the Indian Ocean to the South Pacific. For every hundred Indians who live in India one lives abroad." Since then, the Indian community abroad has grown to over 20 million with people of Indian descent spread throughout the world, with a sizeable presence in about 110 countries. There is hardly a country on the map of the world where there are no Indians.

People of Indian origin have made a place for themselves in many distant countries. An Indian delegation to the newly formed

Indo-German Parliamentary Foundation had a pleasant surprise when they met the German co-chairman of the Foundation, Sebastian Edathy. When Suresh Kurup, a Member of Parliament from Kerala belonging to the Communist Party of India (Marxist) was introduced to Edathy, the member of the German Bundestag greeted him in Malayalam. Edathy explained that his mother was German and his father was from Kottayam. He was born and grew up in Germany and could speak a smattering of Malayalam, which he had learnt from his father.

The international diamond trade was once the preserve of a small powerful group of Hassidic Jews, who could be seen, in their traditional attire, working at the diamond bourses in Antwerp. But in the past decade the Gujaratis have taken over a major part of the trade. Now one Gujarati family can handle each aspect of the trade in precious stones from the diamond exchanges in London and Antwerp to the cutting centres in Surat and then to the setting centres and trade in Tel Aviv.

The overseas Indian community has a worldwide spread, and after the Jewish and Chinese, it is the largest diaspora. It is not a monolithic group, but is formed of numerous layers and segments that correspond to the time of migration, the place of origin in India and the country of settlement. Educational levels, class background, age and gender go to make the other differences. It dispersed over a couple of hundred years, migrants went to Malaysia, Sri Lanka and other South East Asian countries, as indentured workers they went to the colonies to work in Trinidad and Tobago, Mauritius, Suriname, South Africa and Fiji.

They are the children of intrepid Gujarati and Sindhi traders who travelled to distant places in search of business opportunities. There are the first generation migrants who went to Britain during the post World War II labour shortages and to the US in later years. There are the Indian expatriates — the professionals, businessmen, skilled and semi-skilled workers who found work in the Gulf region with the oil boom. There is the last segment, which is not an insignificant one, but tends to fall between all the other groups; that is the second time migrant. These are the people of Indian origin who migrated from Guyana, Trinidad and Kenya to the US and Britain, from Suriname to the Netherlands and from Fiji to Australia, New Zealand and Canada.

Immigrants have a global presence as fresh waves of migrants have travelled abroad in the last decades. The Indian community in the United States doubled its size in 1990s and now numbers about 1.6 million. Gone are the days when distance ensured that immigrants had little or no contact with their homelands. The Indian diaspora has come into its own, from being once known as "the other India" with the connotation of a tragic community separated the homeland, it is now the "Global Indian Family". The Silicon Valley millionaires, the Information Technology and financial whiz kids have given the diaspora a new aura. The Indian Government now honours them with Overseas Indian awards, the Pravasi Bharatiya Samman.

The diaspora includes politicians in high places, world-renowned professionals and scientists, jet-setting corporate heads, top sports persons, writers, artists and entertainers. The Indian media is full of glowing reports about their tales of success, with dazzling stories about their wealth and influence. Indians founded 15 per cent of all high tech start-ups during the Silicon Valley boom time. Indians are the largest minority in Britain and have the highest income among its minority groups. Indians in American have a median income 50 per cent higher than the national average and are the third largest of its Asian immigrant groups. Visiting overseas Indians are feted in India, for they are the new heroes of the youth in India. In death, astronaut Kalpana Chawla became an icon, for she symbolised what a young Indian woman from a small town in Haryana could achieve in America.

There has been an increased interest in diasporic matters in the past couple of decades around the world. Wooing the diaspora is a growing trend around the world, whether it is the Greeks, the Turks or the Mexicans. The 1990s brought a marked change in India's diasporic interest, while the diasporic community has become more enthusiastic in maintaining its ties with India. The "Global Indian Family" is seen as an asset to the home country. The Indian government instituted an annual Pravasi Bharatiya Divas to celebrate the achievements of the overseas Indians and to create a framework for a productive interaction with the overseas community.

Migrant remittances have become a substantial source of foreign exchange in a number of countries, whether it comes from the well-paid academic, the unskilled Indian workman or the Filipino maid. According to one estimate, émigrés of one kind or the other send about $ 100 billion home to a host of countries like Philippines, Bangladesh, India, El Salvador etc. Ghana held its own version of a global family homecoming summit in 2001 to woo its diaspora. In 2001, Indians sent back remittances to the tune of US$ 10 billion, the highest among the developing countries. The Global Development Finance Report of the World Bank listed India as the highest in terms of remittances, followed by Mexico at $ 9 billion and the Philippines at $ 6.4 billion. The South Asian region received $ 16 billion as remittances in 2002, which formed 2.5 per cent of the region's GDP. According to the World Bank report, remittances remain steady even through unfavourable economic cycles. While capital flows and foreign direct investment increase during periods of economic growth, remittances are not as volatile.

Diasporic communities exist around the world. Greeks are a substantial minority in Melbourne while Montreal has the highest concentration of Italians outside Italy. Some overseas communities also dabble in politics; Eritrea funded its war against Ethiopia with money obtained from migrant Eritreans living in Europe.

Afghanistan's President Hamid Karzai returned to Kabul to head the administration after the war on terror and dislodged the Taliban regime in Afghanistan. The Baltic countries had a spate of expatriates returning home to Estonia, Latvia, and Lithuania to important positions in the 1990s. Papua New Guinea had a part Chinese Prime Minister, Sir Julius Chan in the early 1980s. Philippines President Cory Acquino had a Chinese ancestor.

Turkey has a large diaspora in Germany and exiled Croats had a significant role in getting recognition for an independent Croatia. Syria has a separate Ministry that looks after diaspora affairs. The Greek-American community, the Italian-American, the Irish in America have helped to promote their homeland's interests in the United States.

Diasporic communities have come to be viewed as contributing assets by the host countries. By the 1990s, overseas communities had emerged as an acceptable ethnic identity around the world. Indian overseas communities are not unique; they are merely one among many immigrant communities abroad. The United States of America has immigrants of European, African and Asian ancestry; there are immigrant groups of Chinese, Italian, Mexican, Japanese, Poles, Russians, Vietnamese, Koreans as well as Indians. America now has a new climate regarding ethnicity, which does not demand a total negation of ethnic and cultural identity.

There was a time when immigrants were expected to discard their old ethnic identities and surrender themselves wholeheartedly to the American way of life. The greater diversification in the American multi-ethnic mix has changed some of these views, though conformity has not been totally discarded. It is now an accepted practice for the ethnic minorities to make efforts to influence American policies towards their home regions. The Jewish community is the best organised, but others like the Irish, the Greeks and the Italians have also actively sought to sway the American response to the home countries.

The newer immigrant communities are encouraged to retain parts of their ethnic identity and the ties with the homeland are celebrated and emphasised. For the immigrant, assimilation into American society does not mean casting aside all elements of the ethnic identity, it means accepting the American ethos, the behavioural patterns and values of the American system and finding an appropriate place within it. Countries like Britain and France are recognising the need to retain ethnic linkages in their increasingly multi-ethnic societies. Other countries are also devising cultural and social mechanisms by which they can keep alive the links with the mother country. Minority ethnic groups have emerged as acceptable identities that add to the pluralistic nature of these countries.

Migrant communities when they become a significant minority in their new homes begin to gain a collective voice, but in recent times as these migrant communities have become influential in their adopted countries, they have also begun to have an impact back home.

It was the Croats living abroad who raised money and mustered support in Germany to get recognition for the state of Croatia even before the former Yugoslavian federation had begun to disintegrate. Mexicans living in the United States are wooed by Mexican politicians at the time of elections since émigré Mexicans can return home to vote in the national elections.

India is a late entrant in the diasporic search for it required a major change in its outlook. At the time of Independence, the Indian Government had to take a careful look at the status of Indians living abroad—in Burma, Ceylon, Malaya or East Africa. The advice to the overseas Indians was—give your loyalty to your country of adoption. Large Indian communities had lived long years in these countries, and they needed to be protected as residents of these countries after India became independent. Any idea of dual citizenship was ruled out. The first priority for them was to be accepted in their adopted countries as independence cut India's connections with the other British colonies. Through the decolonisation process, as countries in East Africa and the Caribbean became independent Indians had to be seen as an integral part of their adopted homes and not residents who harked back to an ancestral homeland. In the 1970s Indians living in the newly independent African states had to take crucial decisions regarding their citizenship status, and any emphasis on ethnic identity by minority groups in the new nation states had to be studiously avoided.

The lack of contact led to a general indifference in India to the overseas Indians. The later day migrant from India was not seen as an attractive figure in India even though he was wooed for his dollars by a foreign exchange starved government. In the popular image the migrant was part of the brain drain, an ingrate who left the country after a subsidised higher education. He parked his money in attractive Non-Resident Indian bank accounts only because the interest rates were much higher than the returns in foreign banks; but he was the first to withdraw his money when the government was facing a foreign exchange crunch in 1991 leading to a virtual run on the banks.

The migrant Indian was stereotyped as a loud dollar-flashing individual, full of complaints about all India's ills. That view has undergone considerable changes after liberalised immigration regulations and the IT boom resulted in most middle class families in India having a friend or relative abroad. The economic reforms in the 1990s and the example of the remarkable role played by the Chinese diaspora in the economic transformation of China helped to change the mindset in India. Minister for External Affairs Yashwant Sinha expressed the new reality when he assured a gathering of overseas Indians in 2003 that "India has shed whatever ambivalence it might have had towards its diaspora."

In the last decade the Indian overseas community has become

more visible internationally. Many among them have reached heights of success finding a place in the lists of international leaders in their areas of expertise. In recent years, overseas Indians have acquired an image of being high achievers, especially in the field of software and pharmaceuticals, and are now increasingly confident in the assertion of their Indian identity. The rise of a prosperous, confident and demanding overseas Indian community in America and Britain since the late 1980s has brought a change in the Indian government's attitude towards the *pravasi* (emigrant) community. The remittances from expatriate Indians in the Gulf countries became an important factor in buoying foreign exchange reserves. Indians in America began to gain in influence once they became politically active and were wooed as potential donors by American politicians. At the same time, well-to-do Indians were lavish in their hospitality to visiting Indian politicians of all hues, even becoming contributors for all manner of causes in India, both charitable and political. It gave them access to senior Indian leaders who gave a patient hearing to their demands and complaints.

With globalization and the economic reform in India, Indians have been travelling abroad for business purposes, trade, work contracts, tourism and education. Foreign travel has helped the Indian middle class shed its apathy towards the foreign returned. Indian techies and students studying abroad have helped to soften that image, especially as a sizeable section of the growing Indian middle class has a relative living, studying or working abroad.

India is among the world's top ten exporters of migrants according to a World Bank report. India takes second place after Mexico for the number of immigrants it sends to America, while it takes third position in list of immigrants entering New Zealand. The American embassy in India issues about 18,000 student visas a year, of which one third are for undergraduate study programmes. Indians form 11.5 per cent of the foreign students in American universities. There is a similar rush for student visas for the UK, Australia and Canada. The lure of studying abroad and getting a head start in life has over-taken a large number of Indian youth. Migration agencies flourish in Indian towns selling the dream of a life of comfort abroad. With this kind of migration taking place from India, the overseas Indian is no longer the noisy, foreign returned cousin. India is changing from what eminent economist Jagdish Bhagwati called the "brain drain mode to the diaspora model".

Just as the Indian attitude towards the overseas Indian has changed, overseas Indians have changed in the way in which they perceive India. In the post-Independence era, Indians living abroad were cut off from the homeland, as India's connections with the British colonies loosened. The main part of information about India came from the Western press and its coverage of events and developments in India. The Western newspapers carried images of droughts, floods, earthquakes, communal riots, all types of natural and man-made disasters and scarcity of resources. Newspaper columnists wondered how long India would hold together as a nation. "After Nehru who? and After Indira who?" were frequent subjects for deliberation fuelling the belief that India would disintegrate without strong leaders. Overseas Indians picked up their impressions of India from these images.

While the cultural and religious affinity remained, people of Indian descent were not willing to emphasise the ties of Indian ethnicity. To second and third generation overseas Indians, India became a faded picture that existed in the memories and tales of elderly relatives. There was a time when even those overseas Indians who lived in poor circumstances in the colonies, exhibited a sense of disdain for India.

India's image around the world began changing in the 1990s. After five decades of independence and the evidence of the basic resilience of its economy through the process of economic reforms, the old shibboleths of India as a country on the verge of disintegration could be laid to rest. The Western media now writes about India's economic growth. From a disaster ridden, poor developing country, India is now a land of surpluses, with overflowing food stocks, and is among the largest producers of tea, rice, wheat and milk. The Soviet Union's departure from the international scene ended the old Cold War divisions and India was no longer viewed through the prism of bipolar alliances. India's globalization and economic reforms programme opened the doors to a seemingly huge domestic market.

Though China and the Asian tigers of Southeast Asia were the stars of the economic market, India's lumbering economy derided for its archaic controls withstood the hugely disruptive Asian currency crisis that sent the stars into a decline. India's leading position in the new growth areas of high technology burnished that image into a new shine. Its computer engineers and IT professionals made a name for themselves during the Y2K crisis to give the Indian techie an international brand name. A slow but sustained economic growth with several Indian cities emerging as international hubs for business processes, outsourcing and IT enabled services has moulded global opinion. India is increasingly courted by other developing countries to share the experience of its IT ability.

The nuclear tests in 1998 brought down the wrath of the Western world on India with strong condemnation and economic sanctions. But the sanctions were gradually lifted and in the present unipolar world India is accepted as a leading regional power. Though never publicly acknowledged but in private conversations many foreign dignitaries displayed an unstated admiration for the way India handled the fallout of the nuclear tests. Among sections of the overseas Indian community there was admiration for India's muscular posture in declaring itself a nuclear power and facing down the opprobrium of the western countries.

In the global perception, India's stature is enhanced in both economic and political terms as a secular, pluralistic democracy. The new look India has served to revive interest in India among the overseas community. The older diaspora is reviving its ethnic roots and the Indian image as an IT powerhouse attracts the younger generation of people of Indian ancestry. Children of Indian migrants are beginning to feel good about their connection, however distant and forgotten, with India.

The Global Indian family has become influential in different spheres; in several countries where the Indian community is a sizeable one, they are also an influential political force. Modern communications, easier travel, telephones and e-mails, websites and databases make it easier to transcend physical barriers and remain connected with friends and relatives around the globe. After decades of remaining far from positions of political power, Indians moved into the political limelight in their adopted countries. At the Commonwealth Summit in Durban in 1999, there were as many as five Presidents and Prime Ministers of Indian descent present at the meeting. It was a vast change from the period when Indians quietly went about their occupations, keeping aloof from the political mainstream, concentrating on maintaining the family structure.

At various times, successive Finance Ministers have tried to tap the overseas community for foreign exchange deposits. The Resurgent India Bonds, Millennium Bonds and other such financial instruments were floated to attract overseas investments. Indian banks have wooed Non-Resident Indians for their Foreign Currency Non-Resident (FCNR) accounts. The bonds and accounts have been attractive investments because of the high interest rates they offered compared to interest rates prevailing in developed economies. Banks and remittance agencies are now actively pursuing the lucrative remittance market. Inward remittances that Indians now send to their relatives back home are to the tune of US$15 billion a year. While about 40 per cent of this amount comes from Indian expatriates in the Gulf region, almost 30 per cent comes from the United States and 20 per cent from Britain and Europe.

The remittances have increased in recent times as international moves to tighten money laundering and transfer of funds originating from illegal activities such as the narcotics trade have blocked unofficial channels of money transfer. Much of the money that travelled through the hawala route is now being sent through the banks as the black market in buying and selling of dollars is no longer lucrative. The uncertainty that prevailed in the Indian community after the September 11 terrorist attacks in America and the subsequent targeting of some Indians in violent hate crimes led Indian immigrants to transfer larger sums of money to India. Within months of opening shop, the UTI Bank had about one-lakh NRI accounts and was handling remittances worth $10 million per month.

While India looks for foreign investment from overseas Indians, it cannot be the main reason for engaging the *pravasi* community. NRIs who are assiduously pursued for their remittances tend to think that India sees them as milch cows for their dollars. But out of the 20 million overseas Indians only 3.5 million can be taken as wealthy. Indians have been making it to the worldwide list of billionaires and millionaires, but the majority of Indians abroad work hard to make a comfortable life for themselves and their children. The investment and remittance hunting sections may be noisy and even aggressive in their wooing of NRIs but that interaction is only a small part of India's engagement with Mother India's children abroad. About 28 per cent of tourist arrivals in India are of Indian origin. The diaspora is an avid consumer of Indian art, movies, music, food, fashion and literature. Indian films premiere in the United States and Britain at the same time as they are launched in Indian cities.

The diaspora gives India a wider reach in the international arena, through an engagement with a wide range of countries. India has a natural link with the people of Indian origin and their strong desire to connect with their Indian heritage. As Indians traversed and settled around the world, they took their culture with them from India — their values and attitudes and way of life. The diaspora gives India a cultural presence in many parts of the world that helps in providing an economic access to the region. Overseas communities open up new markets for Indian goods. They also play an important diplomatic role in furthering the country's interests in far off places.

There is a realisation in the Indian establishment of the importance of what is called 'soft power' in global politics. Soft power is the ability to influence other societies through such real but intangible elements as culture. American dominance is not simply because of its military or economic clout but also because of the spread of American culture from Hollywood films to hotdogs. India has also a substantial measure of 'soft power' through the attraction of Indian culture, religion, spiritualism and mysticism. Indian films have done more for creating awareness of things Indian than all the official efforts in the five decades. Indian film stars and music have found fans as far away as China, Mongolia, Central Asia, West Asia and Africa. Indian music in its different forms and cuisine has added to the attraction. The Indian diaspora can become an important soft power instrument for it is a potential resource that India can leverage in its favour in variety of ways.

Diversity is the distinguishing characteristic of the Indian diaspora. It contains many different kinds of people, some of whom have absolutely nothing in common with each other but whose origins are undeniably Indian. There are wide differences in the outlook of a third generation Indian living in the Caribbean islands and the new migrant to the US. The overseas Indian community can be divided into two broad categories: The larger category is the older diaspora who are second, third or even fourth generation descendants of Indians settled abroad. The second group is of mainly first generation migrants, who live in the developed economies and still have close connections in the homeland. The term Non-Resident Indians was coined as a category for taxation purposes, denoting Indian citizens who lived abroad. Later the more omnibus term, People of Indian Origin came to be used for all people of Indian descent living outside the borders of India in any part of the world.

The government organised a three-day *Pravasi Bharatiya Divas* function in January 2003 for the overseas Indians. The event generated a sense of diasporic bonhomie, bringing together Indians from all parts of the world. It also showed up the sharp differences between two segments of the diaspora. One delegate from Malaysia described the two groups as the "graduates of Silicon Valley and those of us who have graduated from indentured labour". There was disagreement over the use of the term diaspora. As the New York Times reported: "More than simply celebrating the global Indian family, the conference put India — the brilliance of its minds, the querulousness of its characters, its perpetual grappling to define its identity—on display. There seem to be as many opinions as there were participants about what the conference was for, what the meaning of diaspora was, where loyalties should lie, and what India was and should be."

At the same time, there has been a good deal of criticism in India over the government's efforts to woo the overseas community including the appointment of a migrant Indian as Ambassador for overseas Indians. The growing assertiveness among the recent migrants, demanding political rights including seats in Parliament, dual citizenship and special concessions and facilities, has riled many people in India. Overseas Indians are unfavourably compared to the overseas Chinese who have fuelled the foreign investment in China's economy. India's returns from its massive programme to attract overseas Indian project-investment rather than bank-deposits have been meagre. They are seen as fair-weather birds, especially after the 1991 balance of payments crisis. Overseas Indians, on their part, complain of neglect by the government except when it wants them to invest in India.

There are many misconceptions on both sides on what the Indian government can and should do for overseas Indians. It requires a delicate balancing of interest to ensure that no segment feels neglected. To comprehend the needs of the diaspora, it is necessary to understand the environment in which the many segments are located, for it is that circumstance that predicates what that segment is looking for from the land of the ancestors.

Chapter 2

The Chinese Experience

During the first *Pravasi Bharatiya Divas* in January 2003 a controversy arose over the use of the term diaspora to describe the overseas Indian community. It was criticised as ill advised by several persons, the most prominent of whom was Dr. Fatima Meer, the South African freedom fighter and one of those awarded the *Pravasi Samman*. Dr. Meer said that she "abhorred" the term diaspora because of its connections with Zionism, adding that it described overseas Indians as a people without a home. "We Indian South Africans have had to struggle hard to claim our South Africanness, and that is something we jealously guard. We are not a diaspora of India," she declared.

The term diaspora is drawn from the Greek word meaning to scatter or disperse. It was first used for the Jews who were sent into exile after Nebuchadnezzer's conquest of Babylon. The Jews were sent wandering in exile without a homeland. The Encyclopaedia Britannica says, "though it refers to the physical dispersal of the Jews throughout the world, it also carries religious, philosophical, political and eschatological connotations, inasmuch as a special relationship is understood to exist between the land of Israel and the Jewish people." Dr. Meer's distaste for the use of the term to describe people of Indian descent stemmed from that meaning of the word.

Diaspora was once a term that referred primarily to the Jewish dispersion. It has, however come to be used to refer to contemporary situations that involve the experiences of migration, expatriate workers, refugees, exiles and ethnic communities. It indicates a distance and separation from a society of origin with which there is a lingering affinity. Diaspora is associated with minority and migrant populations that involve experiences of transnational identity. Transnational is another word in use in the diasporic sense to denote ethnic ties that cross national boundaries. It is said that diasporas are shaped through migration along specific routes and histories carrying collective memories and similar identity values. They retain their own distinctiveness in relation to their daily transactions with others around them.

The debate over the propriety of the term diaspora is still hotly debated in academic circles, though diasporic studies have become the standard description for academic work on minorities living away from their ancestral homes. Despite its close connection to the Jewish people and Israel the term has come into vogue as a short hand for migrant communities around the world. In recent times, diaspora has been used to describe any minority community that can trace its origin from another land. The term diaspora has become common usage in international political terminology as the developed countries, which have been the recipient of large scale migrations, formulate policies to integrate the ethnic minorities in their social system. However, it still remains a problematic term for some, especially in countries that look upon their migrant groups as sojourners or outsiders. For, it inevitably tends to draw comparison with the Jewish diaspora, denoting at the same time a transnational motivation and linking it to a common strand of religious, cultural and political thought.

In countries that are in the process of nation building like South Africa, any reference to transnational loyalties or affinities with a lost homeland become suspect in the host country. The celebration of a migrant community is a modern concept of recent origin in western countries. In many countries migrants are still struggling to find acceptance as full-fledged citizens of the adopted land and talking about diasporic loyalties or affinities raises suspicion as it can set them apart. But more and more countries are seeking ways to use the influence of their successful migrant communities. Though purists may disapprove of the use of diaspora to describe overseas communities, the usage has come to stay till a new term is coined.

Among the diasporas the Chinese diaspora numbering an estimated 55 million is the largest overseas community. In these days when frequent comparisons are made between India and China on a variety of subjects, the Indian diaspora is unflatteringly compared to the Chinese diaspora and its contribution to the Chinese economy. Comparisons are made, usually unfavourable, with the foreign investment China attracts from overseas Chinese community. The reluctance of overseas Indians to invest in India is often criticised as a sign of their disinterest in India.

There are, however several reasons why the Indian diaspora has not replicated the overseas Chinese investment in China. The main reason is that unlike migrant Indians, the overseas Chinese are businessmen and traders in the countries where they have settled and therefore in a better position to utilise business opportunities in China. When China began to open its economy, it was the overseas Chinese who made the initial investments and forays into the unfamiliar Chinese economic system. Even now, the major part of foreign direct investment in China is from overseas Chinese, from Taiwan and the Southeast Asian countries. China began opening up its economy 1978 while the Indian economic reforms were initiated in late 1991.

The difference in the Chinese and Indian response to the homeland stems from the vast difference in the two countries' attitudes towards their overseas communities. China has for long recognised its overseas community and utilised their services. India, on the other hand, has veered from indifference to disdain before accepting them as people who can contribute to India's interests. China has almost a hundred-year start over India in tapping its overseas population. The initial industrial expansion of Imperial China that began in the late nineteenth century was also fuelled by overseas Chinese who set up businesses in the ports of Hong Kong, Canton and Swatow. They provided the technology and the capital for railroad building, factories and infrastructure in the country.

China set up an Overseas Chinese Ministry in 1950. Chinese policy is fully geared to attracting foreign direct investment and offers concessions and facilities to woo the foreign investor unlike the half-hearted attempts made by Indian policy makers. A 1995 survey of overseas Chinese in Southeast Asia asked them why they would decide to invest in China. About 45 per cent of the respondents said that they would invest in China for the benefit they would get, 28 per cent added human relations to benefit as a factor for choosing to invest in China, and 13 per cent wanted to invest in their ancestral hometowns in schools and other similar institutions. Only 5 per cent said that patriotism would be a factor in their decision making. Clearly, China provides the opportunity to make good returns on investment.

A brief history of the Chinese diaspora would show that the Chinese migration has many similarities with the Indian migration, but it also has its differences. Like Indians, the Chinese can also be found in almost every country around the world. If there was a taboo on foreign travel for high caste Hindus, the Chinese were prohibited from travelling abroad, for Imperial China shunned contact with foreigners. Unlike the Indian indenture system, labour migration in China was not legally sanctioned by the government. It was the British land policies in India that displaced Indian peasants from the land their forefathers had tilled. Displaced peasants were easily transported to the colonies as indentured labourers. In China, the nineteenth century was a time of relative peace in the country that resulted in a phenomenal increase in the population. The population doubled in size from 150 million to 300 million by the middle of the century putting tremendous pressure on the land. Young Chinese men and women were forced to migrate from their homes in search of work.

The slave trade had been abolished and there was a great shortage of labour throughout the new colonies. Through the second half of the nineteenth century, more than two million Chinese moved from the mainland to the Malay Peninsula, Indo-China, Java, Sumatra, the Philippines, Australia, Hawaii, California, the West Indies and to Africa. The main part of the migration was as contract labour or coolie migration. The largest concentration of overseas Chinese is in the Southeast Asian countries, especially Malaysia and Singapore where the Chinese communities are large enough to be politically significant.

The emigrants were highly motivated people, powered by the wish to make a fresh start after leaving their ancestral homes. It led to chain migration with men from the old village being sent to join their relatives and kinsmen. The chain migration established a common connection between an overseas destination and a village, clan or region in China. The migrants tended to cluster according to family ties, place of origin or a common dialect. It was the pattern that gave rise to secret societies, clans and guilds at the overseas destinations. It also carried over the old feuds between the Cantonese and the Hakkas as well as the bitter rivalries of the Chinese triads and secret societies.

The Imperial Chinese court had ignored the migration that was taking place through the foreign concessions in Kowloon and the ports of Canton and Swatow. But the Chinese who returned home were not welcomed back. The situation changed only after an imperial edict in 1893, which decreed that Chinese emigrants could return home at will. The imperial edict recognised the right of Chinese subjects to travel outside China. It was a change of policy that arose from the Chinese need for industrialisation, when the Imperial authorities realised that the expertise of the Chinese emigrant merchants could be used to facilitate the industrial expansion. Overseas Chinese were involved in opening China to modern mining, railroad construction and manufacturing.

The Imperial Chinese government began to take an active interest in its subjects abroad after this change in policy. The Imperial government opened several consulates abroad to protect China's interests as well as provide protection to the Chinese subjects abroad. Chinese businessmen in Thailand and the Philippines were encouraged to extend their commercial enterprises to China. Some of them received symbols of Imperial honour, granted to them as a result of their donations to the homeland. By 1909 a nationality law had been passed that considered anyone with a Chinese father or mother to be a Chinese citizen. A Chinese born in any country and living anywhere in the world — it did not matter for how many years or for how many generations, was a subject of the Chinese emperor. Chinese parentage meant Chinese citizenship in those days even if the individual had voluntarily acquired the citizenship of any other country.

The overseas Chinese were termed "*hua-ch'iao*", they were taken as sojourners in their new homes who remained emotionally, culturally and politically attached to the mother country. The term was used with respect for it signified inclusion in the great Chinese family, recognised by the Chinese government as one of its own. It gave them official Chinese recognition and consular protection as well as self-respect to the despised coolie immigrant of peasant origin.

The mass of Chinese migrants were labourers, but some went as traders. The notable feature about the Chinese migrants was that they were willing to try their hand at any kind of work. Among the Chinese, it was only the coastal population that was exposed to trading and foreign contact, but when the Chinese left the shores of the home country, they left behind their cultural inhibitions. They looked for opportunities to make a living, fuelled by their need to survive. The Chinese became middlemen and could be found in the remotest corner buying coffee, vanilla and beans from the planters to sell in the market. They were ready to take risks and operate on large volumes at low margins. Their ingenuity and their network of parochial connections through the clan or family provided them the support to take over a major part of the retail trade in several regions.

According to Stephan Fitzgerald's *China and the Overseas Chinese: A Study of Peking's Changing Policy*, remittances from overseas Chinese between 1929 to 1941 ranged from US$ 80 to 100 million per year. In the years before World War ll, the remittances provided sufficient foreign exchange to offset China's balance of payments deficit. Overseas Chinese sent money home to their parents, wives and families, and for investment in enterprises at home. Early twentieth century China had its remittance economy, with many families dependent on the money sent home by emigrants. Money came for building a new house, an ancestral hall, a monument, school or bridge. It was meant to display the migrant's prosperity to the villagers just like the huge new houses with modern features and comforts that dot the countryside in Kerala or Punjab,

Successive Chinese governments, from the Manchu rulers to the Kuomintang and the Communists, have sought funds from the Chinese abroad. They have cultivated the overseas Chinese and sought to link them emotionally and politically with mainland China. After being driven out of the mainland into Taiwan, the

Kuomintang regime maintained its links and the supply of funds from the expatriate Chinese.

The Kuomintang regime had made it a policy to promote Chinese education and language among the immigrant communities. The Nationalists believed that without Chinese language, the overseas Chinese would be lost and retaining the language became important tool for maintaining the links with the homeland. The Kuomintang government sent out a large number of Chinese teachers to teach the children of Chinese immigrants in the Southeast Asian countries. The children learnt a common Chinese language, Mandarin, that was becoming the dominant language in China. Parochial Chinese schools kept the Chinese communities together and kept alive a consciousness of being Chinese among the children.

The Chinese formed a disproportionate part of the business class of every Southeast Asian country, and some Chinese became major players in the host economy. The Chinese system has worked through "*guanxi*" or personal connections. The Chinese migrants have traditionally raised funds privately through their connections. This gave an effective support system to the community in different parts of the world for business purposes. It provided them access to funds and credit required for setting up new ventures or expanding an existing business.

The People's Republic of China changed the Kuomintang Government approach by ending the dual nationality principle. Communist China repudiated the principle of *sui sanguinis* in 1954, which had claimed all Chinese under the sun as Chinese subjects. Overseas Chinese were finding their loyalties suspect in their adopted countries because of their close links to Communist China. They were seen as moles of the Communist regime. Communist China was looking for international recognition especially in its neighbourhood and the overseas Chinese had too useful a role to play for the government in Beijing to continue the situation. The change in policy was meant to indicate that China did not intend to interfere in the internal affairs of other countries through the overseas Chinese domiciled there.

China changed its policy and accepted all overseas Chinese who returned or were deported from Southeast Asian countries. About 500,000 Chinese returned to China between 1949 to 1966 and colonies known as Overseas Chinese Farms were set up to house those who returned. Just as Indians faced ethnic hostility and discrimination in the newly independent East African countries, the Chinese went through a similar pattern of turmoil and expulsions with the emerging nationalism in Southeast Asia during the 1960s.

In both Indonesia and Malaya the Chinese dominated political parties lost ground. The British successfully put down the Communist insurgency in Malaya that was almost entirely led by resident Chinese. An attempt to assert a measure of Chinese identity met with rioting and attacks by Malay mobs in 1969. The Burmese government expelled all the Chinese living in the towns at the time of the Cultural Revolution in China. Chinese merchants bore the brunt of the Indonesian Government's tightening economic policies. The displaced Chinese were taken back by the Chinese government during the period of warm and friendly ties with the Soekarno government in Indonesia. But China's statements acquired a harsher tone during the succeeding Suharto government.

In a paper written by G.P. Deshpande on Chinese overseas and China's Foreign Policy, he says: "The problem of discrimination against overseas communities in any particular country is secondary to the problem of China's relations with that country. If, in its view, Peking finds it useful to remain in the good books of a local government, it has not hesitated, as in the case of Soekarno's Indonesia, to resign itself to whatever view the local government might take of the resident Chinese community."

After the May 1998 riots in Indonesia that targeted Chinese

Indonesians, China expressed its concern at the events at various levels. The subject was raised at meetings with top political leaders of Indonesia. The thrust of the Chinese government argument was that the rights and interests of the Chinese-Indonesians should be placed at equal level as indigenous Indonesians. Chinese officials carefully emphasised that matters involving Chinese-Indonesians were internal matters of Indonesia, but any specific targeting of the ethnic Chinese was bound to be a matter of concern to China. However there are differing opinions on how effective was the "active policy" towards overseas China. The response in Indonesia was that Chinese-Indonesians cannot expect equal treatment as other Indonesian citizens and at the same time draw support from China's show of concern for their welfare.

By the late 1980s a new age of Asian development had set in with the boom in the Southeast Asian economies. It had become clear that the rapid development of the economies of Malaysia, Thailand and Indonesia were in good part due to their industrious Chinese communities. China's growing ties with America and the economic reforms in China under Deng Xiaoping also brought a change in attitude towards Communist China.

The story of the Chinese diaspora is a tale of careful, assiduous cultivation by the Chinese government and a comparative response by the overseas Chinese. The Chinese government approach is that the overseas Chinese act as economic and cultural bridges between China and the outside world. China has had an open policy towards its overseas community for over five decades. There has also been the fierce rivalry between the People's Republic of China and the Kuomintang Government in Taipei for the allegiance of the overseas Chinese community and both have worked hard on the emotional and cultural ties. Most Chinese classics have been published in attractive, low priced editions to appeal to the younger generation of Chinese and to reinforce the great and glorious Chinese heritage and tradition. Chinese films have also made conscious efforts to work upon the nostalgia of the overseas Chinese.

The diaspora was used as the avenue for increasing overseas exchanges when isolationist China began opening up its economy to foreign investment. The Overseas Chinese Affairs Office was founded ten years ago to deal with all matters pertaining to the overseas Chinese. It aimed to strengthen ties between investors and relevant departments, creating a flexible investment environment and looking after their interests. Official Chinese policy has set a priority to involving the overseas Chinese in major thrust areas for development such as the Western China development and Beijing city development. China handsomely acknowledges the contribution of the diaspora, which is deeply satisfying for the overseas Chinese and builds warmth in the ties. An All China Federation of Returned Overseas Chinese helps overseas Chinese to network among themselves and facilitate their relationships with local governments.

Overseas Chinese have enjoyed China's image of a powerful and influential state, which has added to respect and regard for the old homeland. China's nuclear capability, its independent stance and challenge to the West evoke a sense of pride. It does not mean that they are willing to return home, but the power and prestige strengthens the desire to maintain ties with China.

The Chinese government has a clear-cut policy for cultivating and interacting with the overseas Chinese. It has helped set objectives and priorities for building the partnership through encouraging trade, investment and travel policies. The China Foundation is a non-profit, charitable organisation set up in 1997 with the objective of raising funds for improving basic health services and elementary education in the under developed rural areas of China. The Chinese Government has sponsored and initiated efforts to create networks between the overseas Chinese living in different parts of the world. In 2002 a World Chinese Conference was held in Mauritius, that brought together Chinese businessmen and entrepreneurs from around the region.

In Mauritius the Chinese community is merely 3 per cent of the population but it holds a significantly high share in the Mauritius economy. The conference was aimed at strengthening the exchanges and cooperation among overseas Chinese throughout the world, in such fields as economy, trade, culture and tourism. Organised with the Mauritius business community it drew participants from South Africa, Reunion Island, Madagascar, Seychelles and also from further afield like Singapore, Indonesia, Malaysia, Australia, Hong Kong and China. It was an occasion for promoting trade and commercial exchanges between the participants and revitalising Chinese cultural links among the overseas community.

Just like the spectacle of Chief Ministers travelling to the US and Britain to seek foreign investment from the overseas Andhraites, Kannadigas, or Haryanvis is a common occurrence in India, the provincial and township governments in China make frequent appeal to overseas Chinese belonging to their region for investment. There is even a sense of competition between the towns in the countryside with city officials in some of them compiling directories of overseas Chinese with connections to their towns, who can be tapped for contributions. Events of this nature also provide the Chinese government the opportunity to emphasise its 'One China' policy and gather support for its cause for re-unification of China.

Many countries have sought to harness the energies of their overseas comunities, but none have been so effectively used as the Jewish and Chinese diasporas. The Chinese government has focused mainly on economic benefits of its diaspora, while the Jewish diaspora is focused on religious and political issues pertaining to Israel. The Jewish diaspora and its organisations promote the interests and objectives of the state of Israel through its connections world-wide. It is a highly prosperous and well-connected community around the world. It wields enormous influence in American politics and is an important factor in American policies towards West Asia and Israel. Indians in the US have tried to pattern themselves on Jewish lobbying groups in their effort to reach American politicians in the US Congress.

Governments have offered a large number of facilities to keep in touch with the diasporas. Regular conferences, committees to advise Parliament, even nominated seats in the legislature, active encouragement to visit the homeland have kept the migrant communities connected. More and more countries are trying to reach out to prosperous emigrants for a variety of reasons that include leveraging of influence, enhancing an international presence, providing access or prospective foreign investment.

Chapter 3

The Indenture System

The vast waves of Indian migration began with the indenture system of labour recruitment for the colonies in the mid-19th century. As the western imperial powers acquired vast tracts of territory in distant places, the fertile lands provided the means for producing tropical agricultural products like spices, rubber, coffee, tobacco, cotton and sugar. The huge plantations in the colonies, whether British, Dutch, French or Spanish owned came into being with the labour of slaves. Plantation agriculture required bonded servitude, provided first by slaves and later by indentured labourers. The sustained anti-slavery campaign in Britain finally led to new legislation in 1834 that abolished slavery in the British colonies. But the labour intensive plantation operations needed replacement workers and India became the largest supplier of labour within the British colonial empire.

Plantation workers were required in Mauritius, the Caribbean, later in Malaya, Burma, Ceylon, Africa and Fiji. There was a demand for labour for the construction of port-harbours, townships, roads and railways through the colonies. Initially it was met through the labour of convicted prisoners as in Singapore, Penang and Mauritius.

A regulated pattern of emigration under an indenture bond began in 1837 when the first regulations were framed for the export of Indian labour to the colonies. A system was devised under which workers were recruited for a period of five years for an employer in one of the colonies. There were slight variations in the terms of the contract in different colonies. The indenture system was nominally a voluntary contract but many of the conditions of slavery were carried over in the terms of the indenture contract.

Under the indenture system, wages were low and working conditions harsh, even brutal and the plantation worker remained chained to his place of work. Immigration was controlled by the colonial authorities who ensured that there was no shortage of labour that could lead to an increase in wages. The workers could not change employers to seek better work conditions. Initially the migration was through Calcutta port, but later migration began through Madras as well.

Migration from the southern ports to Burma, Malaya and Ceylon was largely for short periods, sometimes under the *kangani* system, and sometimes under the indenture process. The *kangani* was the headman who took a group of workers to Ceylon for seasonal work. The labourers generally belonged to one village or a cluster of villages and returned home after the harvest season was over. Later, the *kangani* became the agent or *sirdar* who controlled a group of workers, whom he had recruited to work on the plantation. The *kangani* would have a relative or associate who would actually do the recruiting. He would lend money to the workers as an advance and therefore get a hold over the labourers. In Ceylon, the migrant worker arrived deeply in debt to the kangani, who kept all the accounts. The kangani collected the wages of his gang and distributed it after making his deductions, but the ever-increasing interest ensured that the debt was rarely reduced.

The initial regulations that related to emigration were under the two Indian Acts of 1857 and 1859. These were actually regulations that dealt with the plying of passenger ships out of Indian ports. The conditions on the ships taking casual migrants to Burma and Malaya was so pitiable that district officials sought to ban any recruitment from their districts.

The British had made changes in the land tenure and food production system in India, which placed the small peasant in a highly vulnerable position. Instead of farmers with hereditary rights to the land they tilled, peasants were converted to the status of tenants, who could be displaced by the zamindar whenever he wanted. Unlike the old system, land revenue had to be paid even during periods of crop failure. In order to pay off their debts or even the land revenue dues, peasants were forced to mortgage the land and many eventually lost it to the moneylender.

Migration was at a high level during 1858 and 1859 just after the Mutiny in India. The turmoil after the Mutiny in 1857 led to widespread dislocation among the peasantry in the northern provinces. The wars destabilised the countryside and many who had joined the army of soldiers and baggage trains chose to migrate when the fighting ended. Many people became landless after being driven off their farms. Indebtedness increased under the unsettled conditions, and failure of crops added to the misery of the peasants. It was fertile ground for the recruiters and more people were willing to move to new places to find work. The rate of emigration was directly linked to agricultural conditions in north India. The emigrants came from the densely populated agricultural regions of the country, and drought or severe floods in these districts would mean more willing migrants for the colonies.

In 1860 the French were allowed to recruit Indian labourers for the French territories. This was followed by a similar agreement with Netherlands for the export of labour to Suriname. A convention was signed in 1870 under which the Dutch were allowed to recruit labourers, for a term of five years after which they were to be eligible for their return passage to India. Both the agreements were part of the British imperial plans, in return for acquiring territory or influence in other regions, at a time when the imperial powers were readjusting their colonial reach. The first Indian emigrants to Suriname reached in June 1873, but the first year was a bad one for the Indians with a high mortality rate and emigration was stopped in 1874. Though there were regulations for recruitment and import of labour, they were poorly enforced. The conditions on the plantations varied according to the individuals involved in the process, leading to some appalling brutality.

The plantations required a regular supply of workers to replace those who had completed their indenture contract. Recruiters had to keep up a steady stream of migrants to meet the needs of the planters. But recruitment was not an easy process. Unlike the settlers from Europe and Britain who moved to America and the colonies, the Indian villagers were loath to leave their homes. An Indian villager drew his identity and sense of belonging from his village, his family and the community he lived in; emigration broke these bonds and was not an accepted process. The famines, crop failures, drought and floods that beset the countryside forced them at times to leave the village and go to the towns in search of work. But that migration was temporary. Emigration to foreign lands was frowned upon in the rural areas.

The recruiters and their agents painted a glowing picture to prospective recruits of fertile lands ready for the taking by whoever was willing to work the land. The rural folk had little knowledge of the world. Their idea of distances was also faulty, many did not know that the fabled land of plenty was across the seas. Few people returned to their villages after going abroad, so there was very little real information about the distant colonies. Fantastic tales and myths were built upon about the Mirichi desh as Mauritius came to known in the northern Indian countryside. The recruiters and their sub-agents used all kinds of dubious methods to fill up their quota. Once caught up in the coils of the recruiting process, the Indian migrant was no longer a free person, his future lay in the hands of others who controlled his life for the next five years.

Under government regulations, all recruiters had to obtain a licence from the Protector of Emigrants at the port of embarkation, which had to be counter-signed by the District Magistrate of the area. All recruits had to be presented before the Sub-Divisional Magistrate before they left the district. Though the profits were huge, a good deal of effort went into getting together a group of emigrants and the licensed recruiters had to use an army of assistants and sub-agents to find people willing to sign up. The recruiter's assistants were known as *arkatis*, they had their areas well defined and kept in touch with a number of informers who would spot the potential emigrant. The process of migration was disliked for its destabilising effect on the village society, so *arkatis* did not enter the villages. They relied on village watchmen, barbers and other local contacts to tip them off about the disgruntled, those in trouble with the police or those forced by a burden of debt to look for work beyond the village.

Village fairs or haats, the weekly markets were places where likely candidates for emigration could be spotted. The temple towns, railway stations, bazaars were places where people could be accosted with fanciful tales. Deception and trickery were used to lure the unwary; the gullible heard wonderful stories of the comfortable life in the colonies. Not many were told they would be crossing the seas, they were led to believe that they were going to some place near Calcutta. The *arkatis* would be on the watch to spot the newcomer to town and befriend him. The hapless victim would be offered food and invited to stay at the assistant's house. It would be a while before the newcomer realised that the others staying in the house were not family or relatives of their benefactor but emigrants waiting to be sent to Calcutta. Any attempt to leave the house would lead to demands that the unwary victim pay for his food and lodging. Many poor victims were bullied into believing that they would be sent to jail if they did not agree to go with the recruiter. Stories with slight variations of this theme were recorded in the reports of the commissions charged with investigating the indenture recruitment.

The Pioneer newspaper, published from Allahabad, carried several stories of people being tricked by the *arkatis.* In 1871 a Baptist missionary Rev Thomas Evans reported the case of a cobbler, Ganga, who came to him for help. His aunt, Ratunia, had gone out to look for work when she met a man who offered her a job to grind wheat. She was taken to a house where there were several other women. When she did not return till late evening, Ratunia's husband and Ganga *mochi* (cobbler) went out in search. They found her the next day in the house with several other women. The women had pleaded to be allowed to go home but were told that they were to go to Jamaica. The men looking after the house demanded payment for the food. Since neither Ganga *mochi* nor his uncle had any money, they went to Rev Evans for help.

When the missionary went with the two men to the house, he found about a dozen women at the house, all of whom told of how they had been tricked with the offer of work. The presence of Rev Evans forced the *jamadar,* incharge of the house, to say that the women were free to go if they wanted. The case caused a sensation in Allahabad, and the men involved in the case were arrested and sentenced to jail. Women recruits were more difficult to find so the *arkatis* were even less scrupulous; plain abduction, threats and deceit were used to get women recruits. The government had decreed that there should be four women to every ten men recruited by an agent. There were some women who accompanied their husbands or other close relatives, but the majority of single women were widows abandoned by their families, or women who got lost while travelling. Their helplessness and ignorance made it easier to coerce the women into putting their thumb impression on the contract form.

The recruits had to appear before the Sub-Divisional Magistrate. It was the Magistrate's responsibility to ensure that each recruit understood the terms and conditions of the contract. It was therefore necessary for the recruiters to prepare their flock to answer any of the magistrate's questions, for he could reject any doubtful cases. The more conscientious officials did make an effort to weed out the unwilling, but most rushed through the process. New recruits were coached or frightened into keeping silent before the magistrate.

The journey to the depot in Calcutta was carried out under close supervision of the assistants to ensure that no one escaped. The group had a number of informers travelling with them, who would beguile the emigrants with stories about the place they were going to. These men would try to ensure that the group did not get into conversation with other passengers about their destination. Some recruits would try to flee after hearing from other passengers what was awaiting them. Even while the groups of emigrants were walking through Calcutta to the depot carrying their small bundles, people on the streets would shout out warnings, jostle and taunt their escorts for selling innocent people into slavery. The port towns had a better knowledge of what the migrants would face in the colonies. But the escorts were well trained in deflecting the warnings and hustling their charges to the depot.

Once at the depot, the migrants were issued a fresh set of clothes and put through a cursory medical examination. Migrants waited at the depot for several weeks, as new groups arrived to make up a shipload of indentured men, women and children. Finally, the day came when the indentured workers headed out into the unknown; crossing the mighty oceans, the Indian Ocean, the Atlantic and the Pacific Ocean to new lands, new countryside, new masters and methods.

Once aboard the ship, there was a complete break with all that was familiar to the Indian migrants. Life on board the ship was the final break with the past, for the indentured passengers lived in close quarters under the deck. It meant a break with the traditions and rituals of ordinary living, especially those pertaining to caste rules. But it was the eating of meals in long lines on the deck, cooked by unknown men that caused much pain and distress to the orthodox. It brought home the enormity of the step they had taken where their traditional values, their religious and caste dictates had no meaning. Some of emigrants refused to eat food cooked in the ship's kitchens, but a careful watch was kept for any one not eating the food given to him. There was always the fear that one of them might try to throw himself overboard in despair. A small boat usually followed the sailing ship for the two days it took to sail down the Hoogly river from Calcutta port; it was meant to pick up anyone who threw himself off the ship in severe distress at crossing the *kala pani*, the black waters of the oceans.

In the days of sailing ships the voyages were long and tedious, between three to four months on sea. When the weather was fine, life on board the ship was tolerable, but when the storms struck, it was dreadful. The hatches were battened down and sometimes the emigrants had to stay below the deck for days, half suffocated by the stale air and stench. The one abiding memory of the voyage that most of the indentured workers carried through their life was of sea-sickness. The long and trying voyage helped to established close ties among those who had broken all bonds with their homes and families. These new fraternal bonds came to be known as '*jahaji bhai*' (brothers of the ship). The *jahaji* bond replaced the ties of blood and helped sustain the emigrants in their new lives.

When they reached their port of destination, the indentured workers were kept in quarantine for some time, before being allotted to the planter. The planter or his overseer would march off the group of recruits to the plantation where they would live and work for five years. In countries like Mauritius the paraphernalia of slavery still survived and the Indian workers went to live in the barracks that were used for the slaves. Plantation life was a world of its own, with its own rules and customs, many of which were derived from the days of slavery. In Fiji, the barracks were pretty wretched habitations; each barrack had wooden partitions to create rooms with mud floors that measured 10 ft by 7 ft. Each cabin was allotted to three single men or a married couple and their children. The rooms had doors but no windows; each had three bunks and a fireplace for cooking. There was no privacy for the occupants as the partitions did not extend to the tin roof, but were topped by wire meshing. The fields behind the coolie lines were to be used as toilets.

Ill-treatment was rife on the plantations, and complaints by the workers only resulted in even more harsh penalties for the complainants. The Europeans firmly believed that the coolies deserved harsh treatment because, they argued, the coolies were used to that kind of handling and responded only to harsh treatment.

There is a widespread belief that the indentured labourers belonged to the lower castes, and they had left India to escape from oppression, poverty and deprivation. It was held that the higher castes in Indian society could not be persuaded to leave India on any account. However, an examination of the Emigration Passes of the indentured Indians who came to Fiji shows that this was not the case. The social and caste data given on the Emigration Passes reveal that the Indian emigrants covered a wide section of the rural Indian communities, the middle agricultural and artisan castes comprised up to 39 per cent of the arrivals, with a significant number of upper castes and Brahmins.

Indian workers survived through the period of indenture through their own determination and resilience. They were bonded to a master, who had virtually a free hand in extracting the kind of work he wanted from the servant. The worker was confined to the estate and was let out only with special permission under stringent rules.

The death rate was highest in the first two years when the indentured workers adjusted to the cruel conditions on the plantations. A system of harsh penalties and punishments were used to make the indentured labourers work. The pattern of operations left the workers open to exploitation in various forms; for the women it also included sexual exploitation. The indentured labourers were given their task for the day and failure to complete the day's task meant that he was not paid for the day. In Mauritius the 'double cut' prevailed, under which one day's absence from work for whatever reason meant a two-day wage cut. In the other colonies a day's absence meant the loss of a day's wage and a day added to the total indenture period. In Mauritius, Guyana and Reunion Island planters deferred payment; the workers wages were held back for two to three months. Penalties were liberally handed down to keep the wage bill down by the planters.

The lives of the women indentured labourers were particularly hard. They worked in the cane fields, looked after the housework, and also protected themselves from the sexual advances of the powerful, predatory men around them. The more attractive women were at the mercy of the *sardars* (leader of a gang of workmen) and the overseers. All kinds of vice existed in the crowded and cramped conditions in the coolie lines. Many widows and abandoned women took the difficult decision to accept a new husband and start a new life. The unmarried, unattached women frequently changed partners and fights over women were common and a major cause of murders and suicides among the indentured community. Several *sardars* and overseers were assaulted and murdered in retaliation for their brutality or for sexual harassment of the women workers. There was no concept of maternity leave, and women were back on the fields with their nursing babies as soon as they were able to move about after giving birth. It was the reports of the exploitation of women that served to inflame public opinion in India against the indenture system.

The workers had no rights as the Lambasa episode showed in Fiji. A group of about 60 Pathans and Sikhs protested that they had been recruited for the police, but were sent to Lambasa to work on the plantations. When they complained to the Stipendary Magistrate, they were ordered back to the estate and the leaders arrested. They were fired up on by a police party, when they refused to work and then taken away to the capital Suva under armed guard. Later they were sent off to different plantations. The administration took a serious view of organised defiance as a bad precedent, and their original complaint of deception was quietly ignored. Colonial administrations did not allow any Indian to acquire a reputation or a following as a leader. Ringleaders in any protest were swiftly isolated and sent off to a different island or region.

Even in the difficult working and living conditions in the plantations where normal family life was disrupted, the Indians tried to recreate and maintain some customs. During their free time, the workers organized wrestling matches, put together groups for singing *bhajans* or *alhas* (a narrative) and listened to reading from the *Ramayana*. The Indians spoke in a variety of languages and dialects when they first arrived and could not understand each other. A kind of Hindustani mixed with some words from several dialects came into use on the plantations as a common language among the Indian workers.

Some migrants returned to India with their savings, though the majority had little to show for the years spent working in the colonies. Some workers managed to save, especially if they attained a position of responsibility like *sardar* or carpenter. Some made money through gambling, others through money lending. In Trinidad, the indentured workers had the hope of acquiring a patch of land to farm for themselves. In Fiji, Indians were leased land to grow cane for the sugar mills. In the early days of indenture, most of the workers returned to India, but as some Indian settlements began growing and opportunities for small jobs, market gardening or farming came up, the migrants stayed back. In the sugar colonies of Mauritius, Trinidad, Guyana and Fiji, Indians became sugarcane farmers.

There were fresh requests for indentured labour from new colonies as well as foreign countries. The experience with the French territories was bad, with serious complaints of maltreatment of the workers. The Protector of Emigrants at Calcutta toured the Caribbean Islands and his reports described the unsatisfactory conditions of Indian workers in the French islands of Martinique and Guadeloupe. In Cayenne, the planters had left their plantations, which had reverted into dense jungle and the Indian labourers were abandoned without means of support. There were reports of grave abuses from French Guiana and Reunion Island. Though the British and French authorities carried on a long correspondence on the need for a joint commission to investigate the grievances, nothing actually came of the proposal. A request from Peru for indentured labourers was ignored by the authorities in India. The Germans also made a request for Indian workers in East Africa.

There was growing unease in India over the indenture system. Letters and reports by missionaries and other public-spirited people gave graphic descriptions of the lives of the indentured workers. Towards the end of the 19th century, sugar prices were at their lowest, and conditions on the sugarcane plantations deteriorated. A system that was already open to considerable abuse became worse as the planters and supervisors cut corners and worked the agricultural labour even harder. In 1911 and 1912, one in 900 indentured workers committed suicide in Fiji according to Fiji government statistics.

In South Africa, Mohandas Karamchand Gandhi took up the cause of Indian workers using non-violent means to highlight their conditions. The agitation in Natal had its impact in India, bringing to notice the abuse in the system. By 1912 the demand for abolition of indenture had become a part of the nationalist struggle in India. The most important event in the battle against indenture was the debate on the resolution moved by the great Indian nationalist, Gopal Krishna Gokhale to prohibit all forms of indentured recruitment in India. The debate took place on 4 March 1912. While introducing his resolution Gokhale called the indenture system "a monstrous system, iniquitous in itself, based on fraud and maintained by force." It was degrading to the people of India, he said, for wherever it existed, all Indians were known as coolies. The debate divided the Council between the non-official Indian members and the British official members; all the Indian members strongly opposed all forms of indenture. Though the resolution was defeated in the Council by the larger number of official members, the debate showed the strong feelings that prevailed among the Indian members. Gokhale had already warned that he would keep bringing his resolution again and again till it was successful.

Gandhi returned to India on January 9, 1915 and by the middle of the year he had taken up the movement against the indenture recruitment as his first big political campaign in India. He attacked it in speeches and in newspaper articles. Calling it a "national stigma", he wrote that it systematized racial inferiority and superiority between Indians and Europeans. He announced that he would launch a satyagraha to begin picketing all emigrant ships unless the indenture practice was stopped The Indian Coolie Protection Society and the Anti-Indentured Emigration League of Bengal were set up to fight emigration. Pamphlets were distributed in Bihar and eastern Uttar Pradesh about the evils of the indenture system and the hostility to the recruitment became intense.

In Trinidad the Working Men's Association protested against Indian immigration as a threat to wage levels and standard of living in the country. In British Guiana, the People's Association opposed taxes that were meant to provide for short indenture periods. The plantations required constant replenishment of labour resulting in an increase in Indian population, which caused unease among the local population. But the interests of the plantation elite were supreme in the colonies.

Reverend Charles Freer Andrews began his own personal campaign against indenture. Andrews was an English missionary who devoted his life to the Indian cause. He had been asked to visit South Africa by Gokhale, where he met and became a close associate of Gandhi. He had spent time with Gandhiji at Tolstoy Farm in South Africa and had seen how the indenture system worked in practice. Andrews described how he learnt to talk to the Indian workers, who were like "dumb, driven cattle, too panic stricken to speak out". He was shocked by the terms in which the Europeans spoke of the coolies.

Gandhi sent Andrews to Fiji to investigate the conditions of the indentured workers. The Indian government was getting concerned about the rising Indian sentiment against indenture but was still looking to continue limited emigration for some more time. Andrews was accompanied by William Pearson during his tour of Fiji. On their return they published a damning report, called '*Indian Labour in Fiji: An Independent Inquiry*', that was based on interviews with indentured workers and planters.

Andrews' speeches and writings that focussed on the moral evils of indenture struck a chord with many prominent British men and women in India. His reports on the condition of indentured women had the widest impact. The wide publicity in India and in Britain had an effect on the Fiji administration. In 1915 the laws providing for prison sentences for labour offences were abolished and the colonial administration directed that the term 'indentured Indian immigrant' should replace the odious word 'coolie' in all official communications. The Governor of Fiji acknowledged in the Legislative Council in Suva that "amid much that is exaggerated, Mr. Andrews has made certain criticisms which unfortunately cannot be refuted." Andrews made a second visit to Fiji in 1917, and this time he was treated with hostility by the planters and even by some officials. It is said in Fiji that Gandhi named Andrews '*Deenbandhu*' (friend of the poor) while he was on his second trip to Fiji. It became the title by which he was referred to by the Indians.

Indenture recruitment was falling for several reasons, including the strong opposition in India. In 1917 government declared that indenture recruitment had ended, but Indians remained indentured in the colonies. When Pandit Madan Mohan Malaviya moved a resolution in the Legislative Council, the government in India, the India Office in London and the Colonies had to take notice of Indian demands. The debate on the motion was held on 11 September 1918; Malaviya concentrated on the situation in Fiji. Indians who had completed their indenture and wanted to return could not do so, as there were no ships to bring them back. But there was no dearth of shipping for sugar and other commodities, he said. Finally on January 1, 1920 the government cancelled all indentures in Fiji and the indenture system officially came to an end.

Chapter 4

Indians in the Caribbean

Indian indenture migration to the Caribbean islands began when the plantation economy began to collapse after the freed slaves refused to work any longer on the plantations. Britain passed the Abolition of Slavery Act in 1833 and allowed a five-year period for ending slavery. The plantation owners made no attempt to ameliorate the working conditions of the slaves during this period so as to retain them as wage-workers. The emancipated slaves did not want to remain on the plantations and drifted to the urban areas. The severe shortage of agricultural labour led to indentured workers being brought in to fill the gap. British Guiana (Guyana) was the first country in the Caribbean to import Indian indentured workers in 1838. Seven years later in 1845, the ship, Fatel Rozack carried Indian workers to Trinidad. The Dutch colony of Suriname obtained Indian indentured migrants in 1873. Plantation owners in Jamaica and Grenada also took Indians to work on their plantations. From these islands small groups of Indians dispersed to the other tiny islands of the Windward chain of islands.

There were several similarities in these countries: a plantation economy dependent on cheap agricultural labour that was initially supplied by slaves and later by indentured labour. There was a multiracial population comprising of the European plantation owners and managers, the Indian agricultural workers and Africans urban settlers; all living in sharply defined spheres.

Guyana, formerly British Guiana, lies on the South American mainland. Sugarcane was planted in large plantations on reclaimed land along the coastal region. In the 1820s Guyana was an important supplier of cane sugar, but when slavery was abolished the plantations went into a decline and several were abandoned because of the serious shortage of labour. The freed slaves fled the plantations to seek easier work near the towns and the sugar industry in Guyana seemed on the verge of collapsing. There was a search for agricultural workers in countries like China, India, other countries of the West Indies and Portugal. Finally, India provided the largest group of indentured workers. From 1838 when the first batch of 396 Indians landed in Demerara till indenture recruitment ended in 1917 over 238,000 Indians had reached the colony. The plantations required a constant replenishment of workers as the earlier arrivals completed their indenture contract. About a third of them returned after completing their indenture term while the rest of them settled down in the new land. Guyana's multiracial population has five main ethnic groups—Indians, Africans, Chinese, Portuguese and Amerindians, who were the original people of the country. The Indians are the largest segment of the population at 50 per cent, while the Africans are 41 per cent.

The journey from Calcutta to the Caribbean took from three to four months. On arrival the indentured workers were allotted to different plantations. Life in the barracks that had once housed the slaves was hard, and any infringement of the work regulations brought harsh penalties. The supervisors and managers had made practically no changes in the pattern of life on the plantations since the time of slavery.

The Indian workers were at the mercy of the European managers and supervisors and their *sardars* or overseers. A daily task was legally defined as the amount of work an able-bodied man could do in six hours of steady work but there were frequent complaints of over-tasking. For the overseers and *sardars*, daily task meant the amount of work that they could extract from the labourers. Fines, beating and penalties were meted out for not completing a task. Absence from work for whatever reason meant the loss of pay and adding a day to the indenture period. The unhygienic conditions of life in the barracks led to sores, yaws, tuberculosis, hookworm and chronic exhaustion among the workers. Hookworm infestation and tuberculosis were a common cause of debility among the workers, which meant that they could not complete the tasks assigned to them.

Once the indenture period was over, there was a great deal of pressure on the workers to re-indenture or to take up the offer of plots of land to farm in lieu of the return passage. Most Indians took up the offer and settled in small villages in the rural areas, to work on their small landholdings. Land acquired a deep economic and emotional meaning for the Indian community as it helped to blunt the memories of the years of hard servitude.

The Indians remained a largely agricultural community, living on the plantations or in villages near their farms. The Africans had moved into urban areas, working at different kinds of urban jobs. Till the 1920s Indians worked on the land and the Africans held all the skilled jobs such as drivers, supervisors, carpenters and mechanics. The different means of livelihood led to a clear rural-urban divide between the Indian and the African pattern of life. The planters and the colonial administration were opposed to education for the Indians as that would have taken the younger generation of Indians away from farming. Almost 75 per cent of the Indian children had no schooling at that time, while the figure for African children without education was 20 per cent. The separation of the races ensured that there was little overt hostility between them but the Africans and the mixed races were encouraged to look down upon the Indians and their pagan religious practices. But ethnic rivalry became sharper when the Indians began competing for the skilled jobs.

The separation between the two ethnic groups helped to breed stereotypes of the other community. Indians were seen as insular people who saved all their money and the Blacks were painted as spendthrift and indolent. Indian rituals like firewalking and piercing themselves with skewers were used to depict Hindu religious customs as barbaric. In British Guiana, the Africans saw Indians as pagans with strange rituals and habits, while the Indians considered themselves part of an ancient civilisation. Blacks have felt a sense of superiority, as they believed that the Africans gained freedom in 1834 with the abolition of slavery, but the Indians became free only in 1947.

The low wages and poor working conditions led to labour unrest in British Guiana. The depression in the 1930s was a period of labour agitation and violent demonstrations. The three main sectors in the Guyanese economy were sugar, rice and bauxite mining. When rice farming was developed, Indians converted swamps and bush land into agricultural farms. Blacks dominated bauxite mining and the Indians complained of discrimination between bauxite and sugar sectors.

Guyana has had a turbulent political history marked with many decades of bitter ethnic rivalry. Race has been the dominant political influence in Guyana since universal adult suffrage was introduced in the 1953 election. The People's Progressive Party was the main force for nationalism, encompassing a wide variety of political views, including the trade union movement. Cheddi Jagan and Linden Forbes Burnham were two charismatic leaders, with differing socialist ideologies, who brought together the Indian rural voters and the poorer, urban Afro-Guyanese in the PPP. In the

1953 elections, the PPP won 18 of the 24 elected seats in the Legislature to the great surprise of the colonial administration, who had expected a coalition government where the moderates would hold the balance.

The Cheddi Jagan government however lasted for less than five months. The British sugar interests were apprehensive of the PPP's socialist notions and branded Jagan as a Communist. A government sponsored Labour Relations Act was the final straw for the British Prime Minister Winston Churchill. The government was dismissed and the constitution suspended even as British warships landed troops for deployment in Georgetown. An interim administration was appointed which ruled till 1957. By then Burnham had parted company with Cheddi Jagan and formed the People's National Congress. In the election that year Burnham wooed the African urban elite to add to his votes and the racial appeal outweighed his avowed socialist policies. It was the beginning of a deepening racial divide in Guyana's electoral politics for the PPP turned into an Indian dominated political party as a reaction. *Apan jaat* (own race) politics became a feature of the general elections. In 1957 Cheddi Jagan became Premier for seven years. The early 1960s were a period of violent labour campaigns led by Burnham and the resultant riots in the country increased the animosity between the two main ethnic groups.

The 1964 elections took place under a new constitution with proportional representation, which aimed at neutralising the Indian advantage of numbers. The PPP had 45 per cent of the votes and the PNC had 40 percent, but Burnham became the Prime Minister with the support of the United Force, a pro-capitalist group that won 12 per cent of the vote. Burnham remained in power till his death in 1985. He managed to woo some middle class Indians by offering prime official positions, but he used the period to consolidate an alliance between his political party, the Black dominated bureaucracy and the predominantly African armed forces. The electoral rolls were expanded to allow overseas Guyanese to vote in the elections, and there were charges of large scale padding of overseas voters list, who voted consistently for the PNC. Indians complained of intimidation by police and the military at voting time.

Guyana gained independence from British rule in 1966, and by 1970 Burnham had declared it a Cooperative Republic with a socialist ideology. In 1970 Indians were 51 per cent of the total population, but many young Indians began migrating to the United States, Britain, Canada and neighbouring Suriname as they found it difficult to get jobs in the country. It was a period of discrimination for Indians as the PNC government tried to wipe out the distinctive identity of its citizens of Indian origin. Indian cultural activities were discouraged, imports of goods used by Indians were banned, names were anglicised and Indians faced discrimination in regard to government jobs.

Burnham was succeeded by Vice-President Desmond Hoyte, who abolished the fraudulent overseas voting and slowly began moving away from Burnham's policies. The elections in 1992 were relatively fair and Cheddi Jagan became President bringing a change in the country's politics. By the 1997 elections the PNC was talking the language of politics of inclusion and both the People's Progressive Party and the People's National Congress were trying to reach across the bitter racial divide in politics. Dr. Cheddi Jagan remained President till his death in 1997. In the next election in 1999 Bharrat Jagdeo was elected President.

The Indians in Guyana were cut off from the homeland during the three decades of Black domination in government. The long distances and the difficulty in travelling, official apathy and even hostility towards the Indian identity cut off the Indians in Guyana. Unlike the other countries where Indians settled after indenture, Indians in Guyana began losing touch with the culture of the ancestral home. Middle class Indians got alienated from India and became more focused on America where most of them wer. for higher studies. The more prosperous Indians know no Indian language; they feel no affinity towards India and are not ready to acknowledge the Indian connection. They have acquired their views from the society around them. Steady migration of Indians from Guyana has resulted in half the Indo-Guyanese population living abroad in America and Canada.

Unlike Guyana's turbulent politics, Trinidad with a similar racial mix had a much more harmonious multi-ethnic society where the Indians were able to retain the cultural ties with India. The first Indians arrived on the island of Trinidad in 1845 and by 1917 roughly 1,44,000 Indians had migrated to Trinidad. The authorities in Port of Spain offered a small plot of land in lieu of the passage home and the majority of Indians chose to stay back in Trinidad. The Indians settled down in their own villages, replicating the rural life in India. Slowly the more enterprising among them began to buy more land.

Through sheer hard work, toiling on the farms with the entire family, Indians managed to make a life for themselves in Trinidad. V.S. Naipaul has described Indians in Trinidad of the 1930s in *A House for Mr. Biswas*: "They could not speak English and were not interested in the land where they lived; it was a place where they had come for a short time and had stayed longer than expected. They continually talked of going back to India, but when the opportunity came, many refused, afraid of the unknown, afraid to leave the familiar temporariness. And every evening they came to the arcade of the solid, friendly house, smoked, told stories, and continued to talk of India."

In the stratified colonial society, Indians constituted the lowest strata of society in Trinidad. The emancipated slaves had moved to urban settlements, they were free men who had the freedom of choice, not like the Indian who were tied to a master. Indian religious wedding ceremonies were not legally valid and children born of such marriages were illegitimate under colonial law. They could not cremate their dead. It was the labour movement of the 1930s that brought some relief to the Indians. By the 1950s Muslim Imams and Hindu pundits were allowed to solemnise marriages. The legal provision for cremation of Hindus came in 1953 with the Cremation Ordinance. The government provided assistance to Christian schools from 1870 but for a hundred years the colonial administration refused to provide any state assistance for education for Indian children. Indian children had to convert to get an education.

The census of 1946 showed that 50 per cent of Indians were illiterate compared to 9 per cent of Africans. The startling statistic led Indian organisations start schools for Indian children. Later, the Indian emphasis on education helped Indian youth to enter the professions of law, medicine and teaching. Indians moved into retail marketing. Some years later Indians came to dominate the professions. They were no longer a predominantly agricultural community.

There was a kind of economic adaptation between the Indians and the Africans; the two communities concentrated on differing areas of the economy. By creating a separate economic niche for themselves, the two racial groups avoided competing against each other. Though the Blacks and the Indians lived side by side for about a century, they had little contact or communication with each other, for each lived their own way of life. Neither group developed an understanding of the other; both used to treat the other with suspicion and a degree of contempt. As Indians got educated, they began competing for jobs which till then had been the sole preserve of the Blacks. The competition caused initial conflicts between the two communities, and over the years the areas of conflict spread to other areas.

The traditional separation in the way of life between the two ethnic groups meant that the Africans did not have any knowledge of Indian history. The hardships of the indentured were unknown or forgotten and radical Africans believed that the Indians had arrived in Trinidad with assured jobs and the promise of land. Resentment built up when Indians began moving to town to take up jobs. Indians made inroads into the professions, but the government jobs, including the police and army remained an African preserve. The Africans gained early control of political power, which helped them dominate government service, the police and army.

Trinidad and Tobago have a multi-ethnic society comprising of Africans, Indians, British, Chinese, Portuguese, Spanish, Syrians and Lebanese. Despite its multi-racial character Trinidad is perceived as an Afro-Americanised society. The calypso, steel band, carnival culture of the Afro-Trinidadians is the dominant ethos and is generally presented as the national culture. Indian music and song were the butt of ridicule in some calypsos. There was a prevailing view that sub-cultures must give way to the dominant one to ensure a homogenous society as a nation building exercise. Many Africans believed that the emphasis on Indian values was actually a refusal to assimilate into a common Trinidadian personality. Indians, on the other hand, felt that the pressure to integrate racially and culturally was a determined policy of the Black dominated governments to dilute their special ethnic identity.

Despite the official discouragement of Indian religious beliefs, the Indian migrants retained their cultural and religious traditions. Several of the traditions were adapted to the local conditions. The Indian migrants named the areas were they settled with familiar names from the homeland. Names like Kanpur and Faizabad indicate the origins of the settlers; Patna and Ganga were favourite place or street names. Indian films and music helped to revive an interest in Hindi among the second and third generation Indians. By the 1980s "*chutney music*" became popular among the Indians and the privatisation of the media opened the way for Indian language radio stations.

The depression of the 1930s led to the development of a strong labour movement. These labour unions formed the basis of the political activity in the country. A number of strikes by the oil workers led to a slackening of the tight political control and brought assurances of local political representation. Self-rule was promised after elections were held in 1956 under a Chief Minister. Trinidad had a relatively faster transition because of the organised trade union movement in the oil industry.

The People's Democratic Party was set up in 1953 by Bhadase Sagan Maraj, an Indian businessman who was leader of the All Trinidad Sugar Estates and Factories Workers Trades Union and the *Sanatan Dharam Mahasabha*. The People's National Movement (PNM) floated by Dr. Eric Williams appealed to the poorer sections of the country. The PNM branded the People's Democratic Party as a party of the rich because of Maraj's business interests. The People's National Movement won 13 out of the 24 seats in the Legislative Council with the PDP getting five seats. Indians in the rural areas voted PDP, while the PNP attracted African support with a scattering of urban Indian voters. The patterns for communal voting were set.

In the next election five years later, the PNM won 20 out of the 30 seats in the newly enlarged Legislature. At the constitutional conference in London, the Indian National Association, which claimed to speak for the Indian community, made a demand for proportional representation in the Legislature and quotas for recruitment in police and civil services to redress the balance between the Blacks and Indians in government jobs. However, Dr. Williams and the new PDP leader, Dr. R.N. Capildeo came to an understanding over the new constitution and Trinidad became independent in 1962.

The PNM was a middle class party, which made no effort to restructure the inequalities in the country. The American Black Power movement had a strong influence in the Caribbean during the 1960s and '70s. The violent protests by Black Power supporters in 1970 led to a political crisis when hundred of soldiers mutinied in support. The mutiny petered out and a state of emergency was imposed for two years. The Black Power movement was a reaction to the widespread socio-economic problems. But Indians despite being in the lower economic group did not align with Black Power, which appeared to them as anti-capitalist, for it opposed private possession of business property. It seemed to threaten the well being of the Indians, who were strongly committed to the land.

On July 27, 1990, about a hundred radical Black Muslims belonging to the Jamaat al Muslimeen stormed the Parliament, took the Prime Minister hostage together with 54 other persons and blew up a police station. The rebels wounded Prime Minister Robinson when he refused to resign. Widespread rioting took place during the six days it took the army to get the hostages released. The leaders of the attempted coup were arrested, but were later released in an amnesty in July 1992.

Indians felt discriminated against as they were marginalised from political power and were already deprived of government jobs. In the early years, Capildeo had rejected any form of alliance, but Basdeo Panday who established his United Labour Front in 1974 began to forge alliances with other groups. By 1985 the Indians emerged as a political force in Trinidad and in1995 Basdeo Panday became the first Prime Minister of Indian origin in Trinidad.

Over time, Trinidad has become a multi-ethnic society with a vibrant culture that is a fusion of the different traditions which its people brought with them to the islands. There is growing ethnic interaction between the communities, the ethnic divisions gain prominence mainly during election time. The main political parties have made efforts to appeal to a wider section of the population, but votes are still cast on ethnic lines.

Across the border from Guyana, Suriname under Dutch control had a different colonial experience. Suriname has an extraordinary mix of ethnic groups ranging from Europeans,

Indians, Africans, Chinese, Javanese, Portuguese, Lebanese and Creoles, each community contributing to its rich cultural and religious diversity. Unlike Guyana, in Suriname the descendants of the Indian workers retained their culture and traditions and the Indian community uses a version of Hindi for common discourse among themselves.

Suriname became a Dutch colony in 1866 as the French, British and the Netherlands parcelled various territories around the world among themselves. Suriname, which was rich in natural resources came to the share of the Netherlands, when the Dutch exchanged their territory called New Amsterdam (present day New York) for the English settlement at Suriname. Planters from the Netherlands, France, Germany and England raised tropical plantations of sugar, coffee, cocoa and cotton in the fertile soil. When the Dutch abolished slavery in 1863, the plantations languished and closed down because of lack of labour.

Initially the Dutch planters brought over some Indian workers from British Guiana. By 1870 it had negotiated with the reluctant British government to allow Indian indentured labour to be taken to Dutch Guiana. Later Chinese and Javanese from the Dutch island of Java, in present-day Indonesia as well as Portuguese and Lebanese were brought in to work on the farms. It is this, which contributed to the extraordinary ethnic diversity and unusual cultural mix in the Latin American country. Indentured workers from Java continued to arrive in Suriname until 1939.

The Dutch had to work hard to get the British India government to agree to send Indian indentured labourers to Suriname. The sailing ship *Lala Rookh* reached Paramaribo with the first group of Indian indentured workers in 1873. A hundred years later a tall monument with a sailing ship was installed on the bank of the Saramacca River to commemorate a centenary of the Indian arrival in Suriname.

There is an old legend among the Suriname *Hindustanis* that many indentured workers came to the country in the belief that they were being taken to a holy place called *Shri Ram dweep* for a pilgrimage. The Dutch government sought to persuade the workers to settle down permanently in the country. The workers were offered settlement rights on government plantations and 100 Dutch guilders were given to those who gave up their right to a free passage home to India. After clearing the jungle and a few years of cultivation, they became owners of the land. From 1927 all Indians born in Suriname got Dutch nationality. It meant that the Indians were seen as an asset to the economy rather than interlopers as they were in Fiji Islands in the Pacific.

Indians were largely restricted to the rural areas till 1914-15 when wartime transport shortages meant that foodstuffs had to be grown locally. Indian farmers moved to areas closer to the towns where there was a ready market for their produce. Paramaribo had till then a small White elite population with a Black majority and as the Indians moved to the urban areas they found opportunities and employment in other fields. Over the years, with hard work and determination, the urban Indians prospered as the better education facilities helped their children to enter the professions.

With the ethnic mix in the population, most Surinamese learn more than two languages, the official language Dutch and *Sranang Tongo* (Suriname tongue), which is the local language of discourse in the country. It comprises of English based Creole with Portuguese, Dutch, Spanish, Hindi and Javanese words. Most also learn to speak *Sarnami* (a mixture of Hindi, Bhojpuri and Awadhi), *Javanese* or English as well. For the Surinamese of Indian descent language became a symbol of their cultural identity. It is one of the few countries, which has a large Indian diaspora where the common Indian language is not merely a spoken language but a written one as well.

Suriname had two decades of self-governance till its independence in 1975. Political parties were organised along ethnic lines, with the leaders looking after the interests and aspirations of their own ethnic group. The ethnic politics led to rising racial tensions, especially in the run-up to independence. Indians were opposed to independence, as they feared political domination by the Africans. Racial tensions rose after the 1973 elections when the Indian parties lost out. The tensions finally resulted in an exodus of Indians to the Netherlands about the time of independence. The majority of Suriname's population lives along the coastal belt with a sparsely populated hinterland. The country is rich in resources and received a generous grant from the Dutch government, but skewed polices led to distortions in the economy resulting in two coups and an insurrection by the economically dissatisfied sections.

Suriname had a series of coalition governments till an army coup by Sergeant Desi Boutrese ousted the elected government. Elections were held in 1987 when a newly formed multi-party Front for Democracy and Development won the elections and Ramsevak Shankar became President. However, Desi Boutrese staged another coup in 1990 and dismissed the government.

About a third of the Indian population of Suriname took recourse to the provision that allowed Surinamese to migrate to the Netherlands before independence in 1975. Netherlands has two distinct Indian communities: the *Sarnami* Indians and the group of recent migrants from India. This community of Indian origin, about 2 lakhs in number, is known as *Surinamese Hindustanis.* The *Surinamese Hindustanis* maintain strong links with Suriname and their heritage as Indians from Suriname. Like the Surinamese Indians, they take pride in retaining their Indian traditions; most of them speak *Sarnami.* After transferring to Netherlands, most of them settled in Amsterdam and the other big towns in the country. These second-time migrants were the more enterprising people and have made greater efforts to integrate in Dutch life with an active participation in local politics and civic affairs. The recent migrants from India number about 15,000 strong and are prosperous professionals and businessmen. But both sections have separate characteristics. The *Sarnami Hindustanis* generally find the new migrants a more arrogant lot, who believe they are the real Indians and the followers of the true path of Indianness.

Indians first arrived in Jamaica in 1845 and till 1917 about 36,412 Indians had been brought to Jamaica. Around 30 per cent of the Indians returned home. On arrival in Jamaica, Indians were sent out in batches of 20 to 40 to far-out plantations. Physical conditions on Jamaican plantations were no better or worse than anywhere else in the Caribbean. But as the Indians were fewer in number and dispersed around the islands, they felt a greater sense of isolation. Hindu or Muslim marriages were not recognised, and after a man's death his property was taken over by the government on the grounds that he had no legal heir since his wife had not been legally married to him. Slowly it forced the Indians to convert to Christianity. Indians in Jamaica assimilated faster into the local community through intermarriages.

Jamaica now has about 60,000 persons of Indian origin. In recent years there has been a growing interest in Indian culture among the Jamaican Indians with a desire to acknowledge the Indian rituals and traditions still followed by many families. Jamaica has a thriving Sindhi community; the early Sindhi arrivals came to Jamaica as traders via the other Caribbean islands. At the time of India's partition in 1947, Sindhi families moved out of Karachi, which had become the capital of newly created Pakistan. Many of them found homes in countries around the world where other Sindhis were settled and some came to Jamaica.

From Guyana and Trinidad, a few Indians went to the tiny islands of St Lucia and St Vincent in the Windward Islands of the Caribbean. A few Indians reached Grenada in 1857. But by 1880 the planters found cocoa and nutmeg a more profitable crop and the large sugar plantations declined. Some owners abandoned their plantations along with their Indian workers. Many of the abandoned workers died, while the rest drifted away in search of work.

Guyana, Trinidad, Tobago and Suriname were plantation economies, which became multi-ethnic societies with the need for agricultural labour for the plantations. The colonial policy kept Indians close to the plantations in the rural areas while the Blacks moved to the towns becoming an urban community. Earlier access to education prepared the Africans for urban employment that helped them to dominate government jobs and the security services. When education became available to Indian children, Indians began to move into professional jobs. Migrant Indian families pursued education with single-minded energy and at great personal sacrifice as the path to economic and personal advancement for themselves and their children.

Chapter 5

Indians Majorities

Mauritius and Fiji are two island nations where the descendants of Indian indentured workers formed a major part of the country's population. Indians were the largest ethnic group in Fiji at the time of its independence and in Mauritius Indians constituted about 70 per cent of the population. But a coup in 1987 led to heavy migration from Fiji that reduced the Indian population by almost ten per cent within a decade. Mauritius did not have an indigenous population when it was colonised while Fiji had a thriving Melanesian population when the Europeans landed in the islands.

Nestling in the Indian Ocean, Mauritius was an uninhabited island when the Dutch claimed it in 1598 and named it after Prince Maurice of Nassau. By the time Mauritius became an independent nation in 1968, it had passed through Dutch, French and British hands. The varied colonial experiences gave the country its multi-ethnic character with several minority ethnic groups. The French named the territory Isle de France and brought the first batch of Indians from Pondicherry to work on the island. The French stayed for a hundred years till they handed over their Indian Ocean colony to the British, but they ensured that the new colonisers would maintain the French character of the island.

Slavery was abolished just two decades after the British acquired Mauritius. It resulted in a sudden shortage of agricultural labour for the sugarcane plantations. The Indian indenture migration to Mauritius began in 1834 and by the time the indenture system ended, about 4.2 lakh workers had been brought to Mauritius from India.

The indenture period was a difficult one, but the relatively shorter distance from India meant that there was much more contact between Mauritius and India. The regular sailings between India and Mauritius meant that the Indians were not as isolated as in the Caribbean. They retained much of their traditional way of life in Mauritius. Though caste bindings did not rule the Indian migrant society, some castes like the Brahmins and a few lower castes maintained their social positions according to their occupational skills. Indian festivals are celebrated with gusto, replicating even regional festivals of the ancestral country. A volcanic lake on the Grand Bassein is named *Ganga Talaw* and Indians trek up to the lake to carry down water in *kanwars* (pots) to bathe the idols in their temples before *Shivaratri*. It has become a major pilgrimage in Mauritius just as the *kavariyas* carrying earthen pots of Ganga water crowd the roads of several districts in Uttar Pradesh in northern India. The television channels and FM radio carry popular programmes in Indian languages, but Mauritius does not have a daily newspaper in Hindi or any other Indian language. Despite the Indian numerical advantage, Mauritius retains the French influence on its society.

The population of Mauritius comprises of Indians, Africans, Chinese and Europeans, the majority of whom are of French descent. Though the Franco-Mauritians are among the smaller of the ethnic communities, they dominate the economy, controlling the big plantations, the service and manufacturing sector as well as the banks and luxury hotels. French remains the principal language in use in Mauritius. The main newspapers are in French, though English is the official language in the country. Creole, which is a mixed *patois* of French and African with a few words from Indian languages, is commonly spoken in Mauritius. Most of the Indians also speak a form of Hindustani with a heavy mix of *Bhojpuri*, a dialect of Hindi.

When the Indians arrived in Mauritius, sugarcane was the mainstay of the economy but now forms less than 10 per cent of its GDP. The undulating cane fields that still cover about half the island, with the black volcanic peaks towering in the background and the blue sea in the distance adding to Mauritius' attraction as a popular tourist destination. Despite being the majority in the country and the dominant force in Mauritius politics, few Indians are in the top economic bracket in the country. They dominate the agriculture sector in terms of numbers, but the big plantations are owned by the Franco-Mauritians and the sugar mills.

As in the other colonies, political awakening and demands for political representation grew out of labour unrest and industrial problems. Though the labour leaders played down the significance of race, it was repeatedly used by the Imperial powers as a means to divide the multi-ethnic support of the workers unions. The social divisions within Mauritius society were emphasised to suggest that the country was not ready for self-rule.

The first proposal for a new constitution was made in 1946 and elections on a limited electoral roll were held in 1948 and 1953. The Indian dominated Labour Party led by Seewoosagar Ramgoolam won most of the seats, the party pushed through a resolution in the Legislative Council in 1955 for expanding the franchise in the country. Though there was an intense reluctance in London to loosen its control, a new constitution was offered that increased the elected seats from 19 to 25. By the time the elections came round in 1959, two Indian parties had emerged: the Independent Forward Bloc and the Mauritius Committee of Action (MCA). A Franco-Mauritian party, *Parti Mauricien Social Democrate* (PMSA) tried to win over all the non-Asian residents but the Labour Party, the IFB and MCA won most of the seats.

There were various attempts to divide the Indian community, initially separating the Hindus and the Muslims in different electoral rolls, then seeking separate seats for Tamils and Telegus. Unwilling to cut the umbilical cord, the Franco-Mauritian Party sought associate status with Britain and other minority communities sought various constitutional safeguards to ensure an appropriate share in political power. It was the towering personality of Sir Seewoosagar Ramgoolam, a moderate leader with strong connections with the British Labour Party leadership that paved the way for independence on March 12, 1968. The constitution provided for a 70-member National Assembly and special provision was made for selecting eight members from the minority communities. Eight members are selected by the electoral supervisory commission from the list of unsuccessful candidates to ensure representation to minority groups in proportion to their population.

Seewoosagar Ramgoolam was Prime Minister from 1962 to 1983. In 1982 the pro-worker, leftist *Movement Militant Mauricien* (MMM) won the elections and Anerood Jugnauth became Prime Minister, but he broke off the next year to form the *Militant Socialist Movement* (MSM). In the four decades after independence, political power has alternated between Aneerood Jugnauth's MSM party and the Labour Party led by Seewoosagar Ramgoolam and later by Navinchandra Ramgoolam. In the last elections in 2000, the MSM entered into a power sharing arrangement with Paul Berenger's Mauritian Militant Movement with the condition that after three years Jagnauth would step down in favour of Berenger. In September 2003 Paul Berenger became the first non-Indian Prime Minister of Mauritius.

While Mauritius went into British hands, its neighbour, Reunion Island, a small island in the Indian Ocean remained a French possession. Reunion had a different colonial experience; it passed through Portuguese and British control before being acquired by the French. Reunion's status as a French colony changed in 1946 to an overseas department of France.

When the French needed agricultural labour for their sugarcane plantations, they initially recruited Indian workers from the French enclave of Pondicherry. But as recruitment was too low to meet the needs of the plantation owners, the French government began negotiations with the Indian administration to allow recruitment in India. By 1860, the two governments had reached an agreement under which 6,000 Indian workers could be recruited each year for Reunion Island. The contract was for five years with a return passage to India. Most of the recruitment took place from the Tamil Nadu region. About the same time, Indian traders began arriving at Reunion Island from Gujarat, many of them to set up small shops.

Indians in Reunion were treated as guest workers, and it was in 1920 that the Indians were granted French nationality. The French colonial practice of transplanting French culture and language to its territories meant that the Indians were discouraged from maintaining their old traditions. They had to become French in language and culture. When Reunion became an overseas department of mainland France, the Indians became French citizens, with all the rights and responsibilities of native born Frenchmen.

People of Indian descent now form a little over 25 per cent of the population of Reunion Island, and are well assimilated in the local society, taking active part in local politics. This has given them the confidence to search anew for a distinct identity based on the Indian cultural heritage. In recent times there has been a revival in interest in Indian culture. Reunion has a few temples though the majority of Indians converted to Christianity during the indenture period. But even as Christians Indians had maintained some of the traditions associated with Hinduism.

Dr. C. Kalaitchelvane, who heads the *Tamil Sangam* in Reunion, explained that "Indians were cut off from India and zealously assimilated in the French culture, but in the last 20 years we are trying to rediscover our roots." Dr. Kalaitchelvane, who visited India to attend the first *Pravasi Bharatiya diwas* said that in the past few years, Diwali and Tamil new year were being celebrated in a big way in the country. There was also a strong desire among young Indians in Reunion to learn Tamil and the language was being taught in some schools and colleges, he explained.

The French West Indies also imported Indian indentured workers to their territories from the French enclaves in India. In 1860 the French came to an agreement with the British administration to allow recruitment of Indian labour for Guadeloupe. But the British stopped the export of Indian workers in 1883 after reports of the high mortality rate among the workers and the poorly regulated work conditions in the French territories. The British had a nominal system of supervision of indentured workers in their colonies, but the French territories had no system of regulating work conditions of the indentured labour.

The French and British colonial authorities went through protracted negotiations over conducting joint inspections of the work areas of the indentured workers. Eminent leaders of the British community in India were appalled at the reports of the frightful conditions of the workers. The British finally stopped recruitment for French territories when no satisfactory settlement would be devised. The Indians, who stayed on in Guadeloupe, were given citizenship rights in 1923. There are about 40,000 residents of Indian origin in Guadeloupe. As in Reunion Island, better communications and easier travel has evoked an interest in Indian culture among the younger generation of Indians.

Madagascar, a former French colony, and the one-time Portuguese colony of Mozambique have small communities of Indian origin numbering around 25,000. Indians arrived on sailing ships to trade in Madagascar and Zanzibar. The Portuguese took Indians from Goa to Mozambique to fill jobs at the lower levels of the bureaucracy. These are prosperous communities, descendants of Indian traders and other migrants over the decades. The trading communities along the Malabar and the Saurashtra coasts in India have long had links with these countries. The small Indian communities prosper because of the spirit of enterprise among the Indian migrants and the fact that the community is too small to attract the envy and hostility that a sizeable minority tends to do in an economically backward country.

Over three lakh people of Indian descent live in the overseas territories of France that include Reunion Island, Guadeloupe, St Martinique, New Caledonia and Tahiti. Metropolitan France has about 65,000 persons of Indian origin, both new arrivals from India and other categories of overseas Indians. Many of them have migrated from the former French colonies in India such as Pondicherry, Karaikal, Yanam, Mahe and Chandranagore. Indians from Seychelles, Mauritius and Madagascar have also resettled in other French territories. Many have joined the French civil service and moved to its other overseas territories such as French Polynesia to New Caledonia. It is generally believed that Fiji is the home of people of Indian origin in the South Pacific islands, but many of the other island states also have tiny communities of Indian origin. One can come across women wearing brightly coloured saris on the streets of Papeete, the capital of Tahiti. They are not Indians from Fiji, but belong to the community of Franco-Indians, who have moved to exotic Tahiti from other French territories.

The first Indians travelled to the Pacific Islands as crew on sailing ships as early as 1811. A few of the sailors stayed behind in the islands, and were assimilated into the local population. The next lot of Indian arrivals were the indentured workers to Fiji and the third wave came as businessmen. A handful of them settled in other islands such as Papua New Guinea and Tonga, and some moved on to Vanuatu, Solomon Islands and the Micronesian islands.

The Indian indenture migration to Fiji began in 1879 when the first batch of Indians arrived in Suva Harbour on the sailing ship, Leonidas. Fiji was a late entrant in the list of colonies requiring indentured labour since it became a British colony only in 1874. The British acquired Fiji when the dominant Fijian chief Cakabau, unable to pay a debt claimed by the Americans ceded the islands to the British crown.

Europeans ships began sailing to Fiji for its sandalwood groves. The sandalwood trade lasted for a decade till the last fragrant tree was chopped down, but it opened up the Fiji Islands to settlers from Australia and New Zealand. The infamous practice of "*blackbirding*" provided the labour for the plantations, as the Fijians were unwilling to work for the settlers. *Blackbirders* kidnapped islanders from the tiny Pacific Islands and took them to work on the plantations in Australia and Fiji. This brutal practice came to an end in the late 1860s under intense pressure from public opinion in England.

When Fiji became a British colony, it opened the way for importing Indian indentured labour. Over 60,000 Indians were taken to Fiji as indentured labourers and several thousand others from Punjab and Gujarat went later as fare paying passengers to Fiji. Indenture or "*girmit*" as the Indians called it was a time of great tribulation. The term *girmit* came from the agreement or labour contact signed by them and the indentured workers came to be known as "*girmitiyas*". For the "*girmitiyas*", the period of indenture spent living in the coolie barracks was "*narak*" (hell). In 1916, C.F. Andrews gave a report after returning from Fiji, in which he used the term 'an abomination on God's earth' to describe the indenture system. Fiji had the worst record of treatment of indentured immigrants and it was reports of the morally degrading conditions in Fiji that inflamed public opinion in India against the indenture system.

A former indentured worker, Totaram Sanadaya returned to India and published a book—"*Fiji mein mere ekeesh varsh*" (Twentyone years in Fiji). The book ghost-written by Banarsidas Chaturvedi gave a graphic account of the hardships faced by the indentured labourers in Fiji. It was translated in several languages and widely circulated in India. Miss Hannah Dudley, a missionary who had opened a school for Indian children, wrote a letter describing the plight of Indian women migrants in Fiji. When the letter was published in India it created a furore and brought Indian women into the battle against indenture. As the opposition gained strength, the British India government feared greater instability in India over an issue that was not directly connected with the administration in India. During World War I indenture was discontinued because of the recruitment for the war effort. However, it was in 1920 that indenture officially came to an end in all the British colonies.

Fiji was in poor economic shape at the time of colonisation and the British government had made it clear to the administrators in Fiji that the colony would have to generate its own revenues. The colonial policy evolved for Fiji meant keeping the native Fijians in their villages and under the control of their tribal chiefs. The Fijian tribes did not have the concept of individual ownership of land; the land belonged to the entire clan or tribe. The early European arrivals had acquired large tracts of land in exchange for guns and axes, and trifles like nails and brightly coloured beads that captivated the chiefs. The new colonial administration stopped all sale of land and introduced a communal system of taxation for the villages. The Fijians were restricted to their villages and their chiefs made responsible for the administration of their tribes. It protected the Fijian communal way of village life as well as reduced the cost of administration. All old sales of land were investigated and only about eight per cent of the land in Fiji was declared freehold, the rest was listed as tribal land.

Unlike Mauritius and the Caribbean islands, Fiji had an indigenous population living on the land, which led to a different pattern of life for the Indians in Fiji. More than half of the indentured workers stayed back in the islands and were encouraged to lease small plots of land to raise sugarcane for the sugar mills. Since the sale of land was banned Indians could only lease the land. They could not, therefore settle in villages, but built huts on the land leased for farming.

There was little direct hostility between the Indians and the Fijians, but the colonial administration ensured that the two ethnic groups remained aloof from each other. At the time of cession, almost half the Fijian population was wiped out in a measles epidemic. The import of indentured workers helped stabilize Fiji's economy and allowed the indigenous Fijians the time and space to recover from the depredations of the epidemics. The hardship of the life on the sugar cane plantations bred in the Indians a determination to provide a better living for themselves and their children. Education became the means to improve their situation in life and the Indians toiled to provide their children an education. They had to set up their own schools, for the Fiji administration and the planters believed that schooling took the children away from the farms.

By the 1940s, the Indians outnumbered the indigenous Fijians. The Indians had become politically active through their struggle to obtain a better price for the sugarcane they grew. Indian cane-farmers had gone on strike on several occasions to get better terms from the sugar mills. The Indians pressed for greater political rights, but the Fijians already governed by their chiefs were not interested in self-governance. As the other British colonies moved towards independence in the 1960s, Fiji had also to make its own preparations. The first constitutional conference was held in London in 1965 where the Indians demanded full independence and a common roll. But the Fijians were opposed to both concepts; they construed the demand for a common roll as an attempt by the numerically stronger Indians to take over the country.

When it became clear that decolonisation was inevitable, the Fijian dominated Alliance Party decided to accept dominion status. In return, the National Federation Party, the main Indian political party dropped its demand for the one-man, one-vote principle that would have ensured Indian political control. The constitution agreed upon underscored the principle of racial balance in the legislature. Race was an important defining element in Fiji's society and played a vital role in its political life as well.

Like Guyana, the other country with a majority Indian population, Fiji's constitution aimed at a distribution of power between the ethnic groups. It also ensured the special position of the Fijians as the original inhabitants of the land. The House of Representatives had 22 Fijian, 22 Indian and 8 General Elector members. Of these 22 members, their own ethnic communities would elect 12 and another 10 members would be elected on a combined, national electoral roll. The General Electors were elected by European and mixed race voters. It was meant to ensure that no single ethnic group dominated and every political party would need the support of at least one other ethnic group to form the government.

For the first 17 years after independence, the Alliance Party formed the government with Ratu Sir Kamisese Mara as Prime Minister. The Alliance Party, though dominated by ethnic Fijians and headed by Ratu Mara, a high chief of the Fijians, was a multi-racial Party with Indian and General Elector members. The mainly Indian political party, the National Federation Party was riven with factions and remained the main opposition party.

The Indians were better educated and well represented in the professions, trade and agriculture, though the bigger commercial ventures were in the hands of the overseas companies or European settlers. Despite all these advantages, the Indian community felt threatened at any sign of Fijian animosity especially after Idi Amin's expulsion of all Asians from Uganda. A tiny minority of Fijian politicians took up the slogan, '*Fiji for the Fijians*' to further unsettle the Indian community. Indians were not represented in Fiji's army and did not own much land. They had not joined the armed forces in Fiji at the time of World War II, demanding that they be treated at par with British other ranks. It was taken as a sign of Indian ingratitude. It resulted in an armed force that was almost entirely ethnic Fijian, making it easier to stage a coup against the Indian dominated government in 1987.

In the elections of 1987 Ratu Mara's party lost to the newly formed Labour Party. Though the Labour Party government was headed by an ethnic Fijian, Dr. Timoci Bavadra, a section of chauvinist Fijians were outraged at what they called an "Indian government". Even as the Bavadra government was settling into office, Col. Sitiveni Rabuka, the third ranking officer in the Royal Fiji Armed Forces, overthrew it in an army coup. The coup sparked off an exodus of Indians from Fiji to Australia, New Zealand and North America, reducing the Indian population to about 34 per cent. Ratu Mara was brought back as an interim Prime Minister.

By 1990 a new constitution was framed which gave Fijians a clear majority in the Parliament by increasing the Fijian seats and reducing the Indian seats. In the following elections, Rabuka did not get a clear majority and had to take the support of Mahendra Chaudhry of the Labour Party to become Prime Minister. In 1997 the constitution was revised with a 71-member House of Representatives of which 23 were ethnic Fijians, 19 Indians and 4 others. The remaining 25 seats were divided among the different communities but voting was on a common roll. In the 1999 elections held under the revised constitution, Mahendra Chaudhry became Fiji's first Prime Minister of Indian origin. However, his government lasted for just a year when an armed gang ousted it on the first anniversary of the government.

After the 1987 coup Indians were removed from top government positions and replaced by Fijians. The Rabuka government's policies helped create a non-feudal, urban elite among the indigenous Fijians. The coup in May 2000 was meant to keep this elite group in power and Ratu Mara was unceremoniously removed from the President's post. The frustration within the indigenous Fijian society was diverted towards the prosperous Indians who had taken over power in the country. The rabid '*Fiji for Fijians*' slogan gave an outlet for the pent-up feeling of the poorer Fijians and directed the resentment of the have-nots towards the seemingly affluent Indians.

The coups and the attendant hostility that they have generated have some important lessons. The present day reality is that the chauvinistic sections of Fijians are not ready to give up political leadership, though they are not unwilling to share it with other communities. Indians are now in a minority and an Indian can be elected Prime Minister only with the support of a substantial section of the ethnic Fijian voters. Assimilation is not the goal in Fiji for neither community wants assimilation. Race is an accepted part of political life, enshrined in the constitution and the political process. Both ethnic groups need to accept each other's role in building the nation as it exists today.

Chapter 6

In the Neighbourhood

India has had close cultural ties with the region to its east, both through the land and the sea route. Inter-marriages among royalty and cultural exchanges took place with ancient city-states that bore a strong Indian influence in their lives. The early Indians took the rich Indian culture to the region; and its impact still survives in various forms in the region. There was active commerce with the region but the major part of migration to the Southeast Asian region began in the middle of the 19th century.

As the British colonial empire expanded in the region, it created the conditions for Indians to move to Burma, Malaya, Singapore. They went as workers for the newly developed plantations, as merchants and traders and for white-collar jobs. There was some movement of Indian workers from Ceylon when it was under Dutch influence to the Dutch plantations in Sumatra. But the British did not allow any direct recruitment of Indians to the Dutch colonies, so Indian migration was entirely on an individual, voluntary basis and mainly from Malaya. Some Indians went from Pondicherry and Mahe to French Indochina in search of work and as traders.

Indians migrated to the Philippines to set up small businesses and set off chain migrations from their home regions. There was a lot of movement of Indians within the region, from Burma to Brunei.

Indian migration took place through organised recruitment to other British colonies, but a large part of the migration towards the Southeast was voluntary. Many workers were taken on short-term contracts with the full expectation of repatriation to India at the end of the contract period. The easier shipping conditions due to the shorter distances to Burma and Malaya meant that there was more frequent two-way movement to this region. Madras became the main port for migration towards the east and the majority of migrants were from South India. The *Nattukotai Chettiar community* had a long tradition of trading in Southeast Asia in pre-colonial times. They became the main financiers and moneylenders throughout the region from Rangoon to Saigon, willing to give agricultural loans to small farmers in the rural areas.

Indians travelled from the French territories of Pondicherry and Mahe to the Indo-China region and Indians became a recognisable minority in the Southeast Asian countries. Saïgon had a prosperous Indian community till the reunification of Vietnam in 1975, but most of the businessmen left the country after the communist regime took over. In the 1970s several thousand Indians left Vietnam and Laos as the communist governments began cutting down on private trade and enterprise. In 1975 the Khmer Rouge threw out all foreigners from Cambodia, including the few Indians who had lived through the unsettled times. Indians currently living in Vietnam are recent arrivals. The friendly relations between India and the Vietnamese government allowed Indians to go to Vietnam to work as expatriates.

Indians began to trickle into Philippines after the American occupation in 1898. The Indian community comprises mainly Punjabis and Sindhis, who maintain a low profile because of the poor law and order situation outside the capital. Migration to

Indonesia was generally a spill over from Malaya but the Indian presence in the archipelago preceded the Dutch arrival in Indonesia. Traders from all over India had for long traded with different parts of Indonesia. Later migrants went to work on the Dutch and English plantations, and present day Indians in Indonesia are descendants of those who migrated in the late 1900s.

India had warm ties with Indonesia but its tilt towards China in the 1950s changed its policy with respect to Indians in the country. A presidential order in 1959 ordered all Indian businessmen to move out of the small towns to the cities. The period before the coup in 1965 was a time of insecurity for Indians when Indian shops were closed down. By the 1970s conditions had changed and Indians who arrived in Indonesia invested in the textile trade and the sports goods sector. The small Indian community, about 50,000 strong is well integrated and also maintains its links with India.

Indians had a traditional role in court circles in Thailand, which got reduced in the colonial era. Many Indians travelled from Malaya and Singapore, others came as merchants from the main trading communities in India—the Sindhis, Gujaratis, Marwaris, the Parsees and Sikhs. They settled mainly in the urban centres and were involved in mining precious stones and trading, particularly in the cattle trade. The community is generally well off, and a good part of it is involved in the textile and jewellery business. They maintain their ties with the homeland, visiting regularly and sending their children to study in India to retain their Indian links.

Indians arrived in Singapore just as it was established as a trading post. It became a penal colony for Indian convicts who worked as construction labour and cleared the forest and swampy areas. Indian indentured labour was brought to work in Singapore, they were followed by traders and others looking for economic opportunities. By the middle of the nineteenth century, Indians formed the second largest community in Singapore, they are now about 7 per cent of the population. The present day Indian community in Singapore is a mix of Singapore citizens, Indian expatriate professionals and a sizeable number of construction workers on short contracts.

Substantial number of Indians migrated or were recruited to work in Ceylon, Malaya and Burma during the colonial days. Though Indian culture and thought had a large influence on Burma in the earlier centuries, there were few Indian settlers living in that land. Indians began arriving in appreciable numbers in Rangoon after the British annexed the Irrawaddy Delta in 1852. Over the next few decades, Indians became the indispensable means employed by the British to run the country. Indian workers were extensively used in colonial times for construction, they were at the middle level of bureaucracy, worked as dockworkers, cleaners, and assistants and manned the police and security services.

As the countryside opened up for rice farming and timber logging, Indians were employed in the rice mills and saw mills. They worked as farmers bringing fresh acreage under paddy farming, they worked in the match factories, the coir and rope manufacturing units. They were municipal employees, manual labourers, domestic servants, bankers, accountants, lawyers and doctors. Rangoon had almost become an Indian town, its trade and commerce, both retail and wholesale was in Indian hands and Hindi and Urdu were accepted languages of commerce.

At one time it was said in Burma, "Indians are everywhere", Rangoon was the place Indian men went to make their fortune, whether educated young men or unskilled workers. Migration was predominantly from South India but there was a wide mix of Indian communities—Telegus, Tamils, Bengalis, Punjabis, Oriyas, Gujaratis, Marwaris and Sikhs. The unregulated Indian migration gave the Indians a stranglehold on most economic activity in Burma. At the same time, the *Chettiar* moneylenders came to own vast tracts of farm land through foreclosures of loans. Burma was part of British India till 1937, but the Indian presence continued to dominate Burmese life even after the country was separated from India.

The Indian dominance on Burmese life meant that Indians faced mounting antagonism as Burmese nationalistic feelings began to grow. There was a periodic chaffing and low-level friction between the two communities. The Indian population in Burma was less than 7 per cent of the total population in 1931, but it was over 56 per cent in Rangoon and other urban centres. For the majority of Indians, Burma was a place to work, not to put down long-term roots, but the benefits of the economic development of Burma went to the Indians. The indigenous Burmese were unfamiliar with the British system nor were they used to vigorous economic activity. Even the more energetic Chinese immigrants were left out, as India became Burma's main trading partner.

Uncontrolled migration from India had created a glut in the labour market and the depression of 1929 aggravated the situation. Paddy prices fell in that period, resulting in an influx of people from the rural areas into Rangoon. A dockyard strike in 1930 triggered off ethnic riots after a clash between Burmese replacements and Indian strikers returning to work. By the 1920s and 1930s Burmese political awareness was rising, it was heavily influenced by the Indian National Congress in India. But the Burmese nationalists resented the refusal of the Indians in Burma to back them on the question of independence. The Burmese began getting afraid of being swamped by the Indians and Chinese immigrants.

During World War II, the British colonial administration moved to Simla after the bombing of Rangoon in December 1941. A large part of the Indian population fled after the Japanese occupation, reaching India almost penniless after weeks of arduous trekking over inhospitable mountainous terrain. A number of Indians remained in Rangoon, which became the headquarters of

Subhash Chandra Bose's Indian National Army. Many evacuees returned after the Japanese surrender to the Allied forces, but the Burmese had got quite used to running the country during the Japanese occupation. The flames of nationalism had grown stronger and Burma got independence from Britain in 1948. Indian leaders had supported the call for Burmese independence and the relations between Indian and Burmese leaders were cordial. Burmese leaders like Aung San acknowledged the contribution of the Indian community to Burma and assured equal opportunities to all citizens.

After independence, the Burmese government began the process of indigenisation in the administration as well as in the economic sphere by nationalising big industries. Indians were hit hard by the new policies since they dominated economic activity in the country. At the time of land nationalisation, almost 48 per cent of land under cultivation was owned by the *Chettiars*, who had acquired much of it through forfeited mortgages. Burmese became the official language and government jobs were reserved for Burmese citizens. Foreigners were given the option of acquiring Burmese citizenship if they wanted to hold on to their government jobs. A large number of Indians left, for many Burma was only a place for employment, others were concerned at the political uncertainty and the restrictions on remitting funds to India. In the early years after independence insurgencies by several Burmese ethnic groups had led to large scale dislocation in the rural areas, forcing people to migrate to the urban areas to look for work.

Despite the pains many Indians suffered through the indigenisation policies, Burma still turned to India to hire doctors in the 1950s. India allowed Burma to practically write off its foreign debt of Rs. 60 crores through supplying rice to India at a rate higher than prevailing international prices. Though Indians were facing difficulties, they still controlled the wholesale and external trade in 1956. The Indian business presence declined only after the military takeover in 1962.

The Revolutionary Council in Burma put into effect the "Burmese way to socialism" bringing the country under one party rule and converting the mixed economy into a state controlled system. All private enterprises were taken over and the country went into isolation, barring almost all-foreign contact. All political parties were dissolved and as a display of dynamic leadership, the military dictator, Gen Ne Win targeted the Indian community. Indian schools run by social bodies like the *Ramakrishna Mission* were taken over. The only Indian organisations that continued to function were the cultural and religious organisations such as the *Arya Samaj* and All Burma Hindu Central Board.

In 1963, the Enterprise Nationalisation legislation was brought in, with the result that banks as well as the retail wholesale and export trade were nationalised. Burmese replaced English as the official language of administration and was made the language for education in schools. It led to a mass departure of Indians, a substantial number of those who had taken Burmese citizenship also left. Under the Citizenship Act of 1948, any British subject who had lived in Burma for 8 years could apply for citizenship. The Indian government made travel arrangements for poor Indians, and special chartered ships sailed between Rangoon and Madras to bring back the deportees. By 1964 over three lakh Indians refugees had returned to India from Burma, many of them leaving all their assets behind.

The majority of Indians who remained in Burma were from the low-income groups doing menial jobs. During Burma's period of isolation, Indians lost contact with their relatives in India. There are no exact figures for the people of Indian origin in Burma, (the country was renamed Myanmar in 1989). According to the report of the Indian government's High Level Committee on the Indian Diaspora, there are estimated 25 lakh persons of Indian origin living in Burma. Between 2 to 4 lakh of them are stateless persons, despite being third or fourth generation residents because they have no records to prove citizenship according to the requirements of the Citizenship Law of 1982. Lack of citizenship affects their ability to buy property, get government jobs or admission to institutes of higher education. The possibility of upward mobility through education and employment is limited and their poor economic status means that Indians have little political or social clout.

India-Myanmar (Burma) ties began unfreezing in the early 1990s when the country began opening up to the outside world. According to the High Level Committee report, the Indian embassy has taken up the issue of stateless persons and about 50,000 persons of Indian origin have since received naturalisation certificates and some have been granted full citizenship.

Like Burma, large numbers of Indian migrants went to Malaya after it was taken over by the British. But India's contact with Malaya dates back many centuries and traces of Indian cultural influence are still evident in the country. The British plantation owners were familiar with Indians as British subjects and sought them as agricultural workers. A steamship subsidy was offered in 1887 to encourage import of labour from the south Indian ports. Migration depots were established and pamphlets distributed to stimulate immigration. The Indian workers came under the assisted labour category, the '*kagani*' system to work on the plantations. Under the *kagani* system used in Malaya and Ceylon, a labour contractor brought groups of workers, usually from the same village or kinship group under contract to work at a plantation. The contractor was generally the headman of the workers and kept them under his control by giving them an advance on their wages.

Later, fare paying migrants began arriving as traders, clerks and other service providers. Indian migrants to Malaya were predominantly from South India, mainly of Tamil origin. As land under plantations increased in Malaya the need for agricultural labour went up; later, as government services also expanded educated

Indians were employed as subordinate staff. Sikhs arrived to work as security guards and in the police and the military. The Indian settlement spread along the rubber plantation areas and the western coastal region.

Wages were miserably low and working conditions were harsh and brutal, and endemic malaria took its toll. Indians began replacing the Chinese workers for plantation owners preferred migrant Indians because they were considered "cheap and docile workers" willing to take wages lower than the Chinese workers. The Chinese were 'free' labourers and therefore in a position to leave an unsatisfactory employment for other occupations. The Indian immigration was from the Tamil landless, rural workers, belonging mainly to the most deprived sections and hence were more docile and malleable.

Immigration was tightly controlled to ensure that there was no shortage of labour that could push up the wages. Unlike the indenture to distant colonies like Trinidad and Fiji, Indians workers were repatriated from Malaya so that the number of Indians in Malaya never went beyond 10 per cent of the population. The workers on the plantations were divided along caste and village ties, they were mainly Tamils while the junior supervisory staff were either Malyalees or educated Sri Lankan Tamils, who considered themselves apart from the Tamils from India. The Chinese who came to work on the plantations or in the mines were able to move out of these low-end jobs in a generation or two, but the low wages ensured that the Indians remained perpetually in debt and tied to the plantations. Their children worked in the fields and they were repatriated when there was no work for them. In 1931 Indians formed 75 per cent of the plantation workers on coconut, tea and palm oil sectors. The Indian settlement spread along the western coast, but more than half the Indian population is not of urban dwellers.

As in Fiji, the colonial authorities adopted a paternalistic attitude towards the Malays. Like the Fijians who lived under the rule of their tribal chiefs, local *sultans* ruled the Malays and there was no feeling of being subjects of a foreign race. It however meant that the Malays did not develop the skills to be part of the economic development.

According to Kernail Singh Sandhu in his paper titled: '*The Coming of the Indians to Malaysia between 1925 - 1957*' the return flow of Indian migrants was more than 80 per cent of total Indian migration to Malaya in the year. Most Indians were seasonal migrants, who came on short-term contracts. By 1938 the British India government had banned all assisted emigration of unskilled labour from India. The majority of the Indian community was plantation workers, who remained a poor, landless rural class, lagging behind in education and economic progress. Some were middle class professionals, teachers and businessmen. In 1957 the Indian population in Malaysia was 820,270 of which 62 per cent was local born.

Indians remained on the periphery in politics because of their numbers. Indians were about 7 per cent of the electorate compared to 36 per cent Chinese and 55 per cent Malays. The Malayan Indian Congress was established in 1946; it aligned with the ruling coalition, National Front (Barisan National) getting some party and government positions in return for their support. Indian leaders had also been active in the opposition politics in the pre-1969 period. The radicalisation of politics after the 1969 riots led to the opposition parties getting more communally activated. The MIC became the main voice of the Indian community, but its leaders were not able to leverage their position in government for the benefit of the community. Caste and factionalism were a frequent part of MIC politics.

Indians in Malaya were squeezed between the Malays who were asserting their indigenous rights as *bhumiputras* (sons of the soil) and the assertive Chinese immigrants. By the 1930s, about 25 per cent of land was reserved for Malays, and the tea, coconut, palm oil plantations covered large tracts of cultivatable land. Indians had to compete with the more aggressive Chinese to acquire small land holdings. The Chinese had a better capacity to save and could get credit and marketing facilities through the Chinese retail network.

In the multi-racial society, each ethnic group had its set of grievances. The Malays saw themselves as victims for economic power was concentrated in the hands of the Chinese immigrants. The Chinese, on the other hand, felt deprived of real power and the full rights of residence. Between the two major communities, the Indians felt their interests were ignored and marginalised. The New Economic Policy (NEP) of the 1970s was formulated to establish the Malay dominance in political affairs as well as correct the economic imbalance. It began by enhancing their share in the country's economic and administrative sectors. The Indians stayed at the bottom of the ladder. They were mainly employed in the plantations, a few held senior level positions in government service, others were blue-collar workers in the public works, railways etc.

The new constitution gave specific guarantees to the special privileges that were given to the Malays. The citizenship laws were revised and anyone born in Malaya after independence automatically became a citizen, but had to specifically renounce all claims to citizenship in other lands, such as India or China. Thousands of plantation workers became stateless even when Malay born for many failed to register themselves as citizens due to ignorance.

Indians were the worst affected by the *bhumiputra* (son of the soil) policies, which restricted their economic and job opportunities. Indians are the junior partners in the ethnic mix in Malaysian society, but many indigenous Malays feel that Indians have very strong emotional and political attachments to India. Though there is general ethnic harmony, but some recent violent incidents did create disquiet among Indians in Malaysia. The Indian community in Malaysia is about 1.6 million strong, and forms around 7 per cent of the population. There are around 50,000 stateless persons of Indian origin in the country, who are still to be granted Malaysian citizenship.

Migrant Indians went to Burma and Malaya during the colonial period but there were several waves of migration from Tamil Nadu to Ceylon through the ages. Tamils settled in the Jaffna peninsula, and are known as Sri Lankan Tamils after Ceylon was renamed Sri Lanka after independence. Tamil plantation workers form an entirely separate category who live in the plantation areas of central Sri Lanka. They have little to do with the Sri Lankan Tamils, living in a different part of the country with different concerns and problems.

In the early nineteenth century, Indian migrants began going to Ceylon to work on the Dutch cinnamon plantations. A regular inflow of migrants began in the 1830s to work on the coffee estates, increasing in numbers when fresh areas came under tea and rubber plantations in the 1880s. The coffee estates required seasonal labour, the workers came from southern India and returned home after the harvest season ended. The tea and rubber estates required labour throughout the year, with the result that the workers stayed on the plantations. Families came out to join the workers for there was picking work available for women and children. It changed the pattern of migration, though the proximity of the homeland still made it a fairly mobile labour group. Many migrant workers returned home after some years of working on the Ceylonese plantations.

Till 1931 the Indians were guest workers but when Ceylon got a new constitution that year, it raised the question of the status of the Indian workers. It was about the same time that economic recession hit the island economy, and jobs were scarce for everyone. Migrant workers and minorities are generally the worst affected during an economic downturn, while they face the hostility of the majority community for taking away the jobs. Sinhala leaders tried to ensure that some types of economic activity be reserved only for the Sinhalas. The majority of the Indian migrants were estate workers and their families, but there were others who were traders, professionals and urban workers. Though only a small segment in Ceylon's population, the Indian migrants not only dominated the labour market but also the important sections of the economy. Just before independence, Indian merchants and retailers dominated the non-European segment of Ceylon's economy while the *Chettiar* moneylenders had acquired vast acreage of coconut plantations through debt recovery.

The Tamils in the Jaffna peninsula were Sri Lankan nationals, but the plantation Tamils faced problems in meeting the new citizenship requirements. The Tamil plantation workers had voted in the 1931, 1936 and 1947 elections, but their citizenship status came into question after Ceylon became independent. Under the new laws, the names of almost all Tamil workers were deleted from the electoral rolls and most of them had to apply for citizenship. The majority of plantation workers were unwilling to opt for Indian citizenship, but only a small number qualified for Sri Lankan citizenship. A large number of Tamils were classified as 'stateless', most of them lived in the rural areas. Strong public opinion in Tamil Nadu ensured that the Indian government could not ignore the post-independence events in Sri Lanka, even though it took the official position that they were not India's responsibility.

The newly independent Sri Lankan government was loath to take any action against the "stateless" workers. Expelling the Tamil workers was not feasible for it would have led to severe labour shortage on the plantations as well as have a damaging impact on India-Sri Lankan relations. Tea and rubber were the two dominant sectors of the Ceylonese economy, and Indians formed almost 80 per cent of the labour force on the tea and rubber estates. The Sinhalese, like the indigenous population in other British colonies where migrant workers had been imported, were unwilling to work on the estates.

Under the two Indo-Sri Lankan pacts of 1964 and 1974 stateless persons were to be granted Sri Lankan citizenship or repatriated to India according to an agreed proportionate ratio. But neither of the agreements were successfully implemented. About 1.3 lakh Indians had returned to Tamil Nadu by 1964 and another 3.4 lakhs returned later. In August 2003, the Sri Lankan government announced its decision to grant citizenship to 1.68 lakh persons of Indian origin living in Sri Lanka. They are part of the one million persons of Indian origin, mainly Tamils who became stateless at the time of Sri Lanka's independence in 1948.

Chapter 7

The African Experience

India has traded with East Africa for centuries, through Zanzibar and along the coast with the traditional ports of Mombasa and Dar es Salaam. Ibn Batuta wrote about Mombasa as a big town in the 1300s and Vasco de Gama found it a thriving commercial centre with merchants from as far as Calicut and the western Indian coast. Indians held important positions in the administration of the Arab *sultanate* (kingdom) of Zanzibar. The age old trading contacts turned into a regular migration during the colonial period.

Dutch records show that there were Indians in South Africa shortly after they established a settlement in the Cape in 1652. The Dutch took Indians as servants from India and the East Indies and sold them as slaves in the Cape colony on their way home. The Indians were a significant presence in the early days of the settlement but got assimilated in the colony over the years and left no trace of their separate identity. Large scale Indian migration to South Africa began when the indenture system was extended to South Africa. Natal had adopted a mix of the two prevalent forms of colonial settlement—the Australian pattern that obtained a

White work force through assisted migration from European countries, and the plantation type of settlement of importing a black labour force.

The Natal area required a large number of replacement workers for its newly settled sugar, coffee and cotton plantations. But it took some time for the India government to agree to Natal's request after a long round of negotiations on the indenture conditions. The first ship from Madras, the S.S. Truro arrived at Durban carrying Indian indentured labourers on November 16, 1860. When the Indians arrived, Natal was practically on the verge of bankruptcy. However, the Indian government stopped immigration after it received reports from returned migrants of the harsh treatment at the farms in Natal. Immigration was only revived in 1874 after the Natal government accepted some of the recommendations of a commission appointed to look into the conditions of the immigrants. Migration to Natal took place mainly from the southern Indian ports.

By the 1890s the Indian population in Natal had increased at a rapid pace for the plantations needed regular replenishment of farm workers. After completing their indenture term, Indians looked for work on the railways, the dockyards, coalmines and public works; they took to small jobs, market gardening, and became petty traders and hawkers. Most Indians stayed in Natal while a few thousand moved into neighbouring Transvaal. The indentured Indians were followed by the "free" or "passage" Indians, who took up jobs as teachers, accountants and lawyers. Traders from India and Mauritius came to do business in Natal and it was not long before the White settlers began to resent the Indian foray into trading, which was cutting into their profits.

Over one and a half lakh Indians migrated to South Africa in the next five decades, till the Europeans began feeling outnumbered by the Indians. An anti-Indian sentiment was generated especially among the small shopkeepers who were directly affected by Indian competition. The growing hostility spread through the White settler community, who proposed that only indentured Indians should be allowed to stay in Natal.

A poll tax of 3 pounds was imposed on Indians who stayed on in Natal after completing their indenture term. In earlier years Indians had the right to vote, but in 1894 the Natal government took away the right to vote from the Indians. It was the year when a lawyer from India, Mohandas Karamchand Gandhi set up the Natal Indian Congress. One of the organisation's first tasks was to collect signatures of almost all "free" Indians to petition the British Secretary of State for the Colonies to protest their disenfranchisement. The Natal Government then sought other means to keep the Indians off the voters list and introduced the Immigration Restriction Act which required all immigrants from India to be proficient in writing a European language.

In their petition Indian leaders suggested that indentured immigration should be stopped. It was not a suggestion that the Natal authorities were ready to accept for they continued to write to the government in India and the Colonial Office in London for further immigration under revised rules. After the end of the Anglo-Boer war between the British and the descendants of the Dutch settlers, industrial activity had resumed and the need for labour had grown enormously. In 1902 the governor of Natal wrote to India for relaxation in the rules for recruitment to meet the increased demand for workers in the coalmines. It was the same year in which the Natal government extended the poll tax to include minors and children.

The difficulties faced by the Indians in South Africa began to create ripples in India. Leaders like Dadabhai Naoroji took up the subject of the high rate of suicides among the indentured labourers. The Indian National Congress meeting in Varanasi in 1905 passed a resolution protesting against the denial of citizenship to Indians and called upon the government in India to stop all emigration to South Africa.

In 1906 the four colonies of Natal, Cape Town, Transvaal and Orange Free State formed a union that became present day South Africa. Orange Free State barred entry of Indians in its territory and Transvaal passed the Asiatic Law Amendment Ordinance that required Indians over the age of eight years to register with the Registrar of Asiatics. The registration certificate had to be carried at all times and failure to produce it on demand attracted a fine of 100 pounds, three months imprisonment or deportation to India. The Indian community formed the Passive Resistance Association to oppose what came to be called the Black Act. It was the first time that Gandhi devised and used non-cooperation as a strategy to oppose an unjust law. Indians picketed the Registrar's office and refused to register themselves.

A Supreme Court order ruled that marriages conducted under Indian religious ceremonies were not legal, rendering all Indian marriages invalid. The anti-Indian judgement brought out women protestors to join the agitation. The brutality with which a group of miners marching to Transvaal were treated led to a general strike of Indian workers in Natal. It was the first political strike in South Africa. The strike eventually led to the setting up of a Commission whose recommendations formed part of the Indian Relief Bill of 1914. The legislation abolished the poll tax, validated Indian marriages and allowed families of Indian workers to join them in South Africa.

However, it was a short-lived respite, for harassment of Indians began after the World War I ended. There were demands that Indians be repatriated, and efforts were made to segregate the Indian community in Natal and to boycott Indian traders. Regulations had been brought in by the early 1920s to forbid land and property owners from selling to Indian buyers. During the years of depression, laws were adopted reserving some types of jobs for workers of European origin. The depression led to increased migration from the rural areas to the towns; the poorer Whites came looking for work and new laws were enacted to help them at the cost of Indian workers.

By 1931 the younger sections of the Indian community became more aggressive in responding to the harassment. Younger Indians, whose parents came to South Africa as indentured workers, were more determined in their opposition to discriminatory practices. They were not willing to be led by the moderates, who were mainly traders and professionals. They set up new groups trying to make common cause with Africans and the progressive sections among the White community. The Pegging Act of 1943 marked out Indian areas and forbade the purchase and occupation of land by Indians outside the designated areas.

The Nationalist Party came to power with the most reactionary whites as its dominating force. The Afrikaners who believed that South Africa was a God-given land and they had to make it their own, devised the apartheid system. The racial groups had to be segregated and Africans had to be sent off to specific areas called 'homelands'. The Group Areas Act was passed in 1950 for total separation of the racial groups in urban areas. The Africans already lived in shantytowns but the Act hit the Indian traders and professionals, who were driven out from prime land in the centre of town to the outskirts.

The Asiatic Land Tenure and Indian Representation Act of 1946 legalising the principle of segregation of Asiatics and the race riots in Durban in January 1949 were major turning points for the Indians. It had become clear that Indians could not remain isolated or neutral in the larger battle in South Africa; they had to move in co-ordination with the Africans. Indians did not support the racist policies but in the early years their problems were different as compared to the Africans who were already victims of segregation. The government tried to play one community against another. It was when the segregation policy came to be applied to the Indians that the Indian leaders began coordinating with the African opposition.

As the Indians came under greater pressure, they found more common grounds with the Africans and slowly the unity among the leaders of both communities began to seep through in wider circles. Both communities were opposed to the government regulations and planned joint campaigns against them. They jointly began the Defiance Campaign in 1952 that was the first major protest movement comprising all racial groups. In 1955 a National Congress of the people was held in Johannesburg that drafted the Freedom Charter, which voiced the demands and aspirations of the people of South Africa. The Government charged the leaders of the Congress with treason, the trials went on for five years till all those charged were acquitted, but the trials used up a great deal of energy, time and money.

The Indian Government broke off all ties with the South African apartheid regime in 1955. There was no official connection between the two countries, which added to the isolation of the Indian community in South Africa. The situation was exacerbated after the African National Conference opened an office in New Delhi. In South Africa it was not British colonialism at work but an entrenched minority, racist regime. South Africa became a Republic on May 31, 1961, and in 1962 Indians were granted permanent resident status.

The majority of the Whites in South Africa did not consider Indians as a part of the South African nation, but as sojourners. The government in the newly formed Republic, however, declared that the Indians were an integral part of the country. In actual fact, most of the Indians were already legal citizens with documents such as passports, listing in the census and identity cards. Any attempt to revoke the citizenship papers of the Indian residents would have had international repercussions. Under sustained attack at the United Nations, the South African Permanent Representative to the UN stated that his government had given up its long cherished plan to repatriate the Indians from South Africa. The government constituted a Department for Indian Affairs and an Indian bank was established which provided credit facilities to Indians for setting up small enterprises.

The Government decided to set up a council of Indians in 1964 that could be consulted on various subjects like education, religion, business, industry and labour pertaining to the Indian community. It was said that the council could at a later stage become an elected body. But the majority of Indian leaders opposed the concept on the grounds that the council would put an end to any possibility of Indian representation on governing institutions. The Indian community was opposed to the policy of separate development of racial groups. But when the council was constituted several prominent Indians were persuaded through various means to join it. The South African Indian Council had no powers and merely acted as an advisory body for the Minister for Indian Affairs.

Indians opposed the separate university for Indians, but later acquiesced, as it was the only avenue for higher education open to the community. In a powerless minority community with no hope of redressal against discrimination, some individuals have often aligned with the power wielders as a means of survival. In 1982 a Tricameral Parliament was constituted for the Whites, the Coloureds and the Indians. Blacks had no representation in Parliament. The Natal Indian Congress and the Transvaal Indian Congress launched a campaign to boycott elections to the Parliament but the presence of a few Indians in the legislature obscured the Indian resistance to the policies of racial segregation.

While the Indians were finding some form of livelihood, the Africans had even fewer avenues for employment. Government policy placed severe restrictions on any contacts between Indians and the Africans, except in a commercial setting. The Afrikaans exploited misunderstandings, envy and jealousies between the two groups, diverting resentment towards Indian shopkeepers and small business owners for making easy profits.

The Indian community had some sections that were immensely rich, who lived a life of opulent luxury. They made no bones of the fact that they were well satisfied with their lifestyles that kept them insulated from the local Africans. Indians joined the joint campaign of strikes and demonstrations against the racist regime and several politically active Indians became close associates of ANC leaders in jail. But the majority of the Indian community lived in Durban in the Kwazulu land, and fearing African domination and hostility, chose to be politically apathetic.

In February 1990 President F.W. De Klerk made his speech announcing the end of apartheid. But the transition to a non-racial democracy was a tense period as intra-Black violence spread through the townships. It was a difficult time for the Indians who feared that they would also become victims of the violence. However, the ANC and the Inkatha Freedom Party finally signed an agreement, which sought to eliminate all forms of racial discrimination for "South Africa belongs to all who live in it".

African National Congress leader Nelson Mandela offered all assurances to the Indian community when he became President of South Africa. Mandela's first Cabinet included five Cabinet Ministers of Indian origin. When Molvi Ahmed Cachalia, one of the leaders of 1952 Defiance Campaign and a long time associate of Walter Sisulu, died in August 2003 at the age of 95 years, Nelson Mandela described him as one of the pillars that united South Africa.

However, the majority of the Indian community voted for de Klerk's National Party to the dismay of the Indian leaders in the ANC. In the 1999 elections, the Indians voted for the newly formed White dominated Democratic Alliance. The Indian voting pattern riled the ANC leaders resulting in a shift in perception about the Indians when Thabo Mbeki took over as President from Nelson Mandela in 1999. A decade after the end of the racist political structure the process of nation building continues and the Indian community has to find ways to visibly integrate in the new multi-racial society. The majority of the Indian community (about 80 per cent) live in Durban area, and more than 60 per cent of the community are poor or unemployed. The high crime rate and the periodic eruptions of anti-Indian feelings tend to keep the community on edge.

In South Africa Indian workers were brought to save the plantation economy from collapse, while Indians were taken to East Africa for the construction of a cross African railroad connecting Mombasa on the Kenyan coast to Uganda's capital, Kampala. The intrepid Indian workers cleared the jungle, laid the tracks for the railway and opened up the interior regions. They faced a variety of difficult situations, from rampaging lions and other jungle encounters to unfamiliar diseases that killed large number of workers. The construction work also brought along an army of service providers: peddlers, traders, and small shopkeepers catering to the needs of the railway workers. Many of them stayed on after the construction workers returned home.

It was the Asians who opened up the interior of the East African region to white settlers, playing a crucial role in the economic development of the region. They helped market the local crops when Indian traders travelled to remote villages with their boxes of colourful goods, bought the local produce and transported it to the coastal areas. An East African Economic Commission report of 1917 stated that "the Indian plays a useful part in opening up trade, stimulating the wants of the natives and inducing them to part with their products for purposes of export." It was the Asians who set up little shops or *dukas* as they were known in the rural areas, subsisting on the small returns they made on their goods. From the small beginnings, the Asians went on to professional and middle-level jobs. Later, they provided the skilled workers and artisans, as well as the professionals in engineering, medicine, law and accountancy as also the junior and middle level managers.

Aside from being an integral part of the rural retail, distribution and purchase chain, the Asians with their propensity to save, built up small amounts of capital that was invested in productive sectors of the economy. Winston Churchill in his book, "*My African Journey*" said that it was the Indian trader who developed the early beginnings of trade and opened up the first slender means of communication to all sorts of places to which no white man would go or earn a living. Churchill said that it was the Indian banker who supplied the larger part of the capital for business and enterprise to the White settler and the Indian trader.

The Indian settlement in Africa during the colonial period was mainly in countries with a sizeable European population. The European-Indian migration led to a hierarchically configured pyramid where the Africans formed the base, Indians placed in the middle and the Europeans at the uppermost level of society. Designated residential areas, schools and hospitals, with clearly defined no-go areas and a separate salary structure reinforced the segregation between the races. Unlike the early Indian indentured workers in the Caribbean islands who were placed at the bottom of the social heap, the policies in Africa preserved the privileges of the Europeans, with the Asians as a service community and the Africans at the bottom rung. The Asians lived in social isolation with their own schools, clubs and religious organisations. Their status and privileges were marginally better. Though they did not enjoy the prestige of the colonial masters, they acquired the opprobrium of aligning with the oppressors.

The crucial factor in Africa has been the lack of economic opportunities for Africans and they have tended to blame the alien communities for their economic backwardness. The colonial period was a time of exploitation and deprivation for the Africans, so it was natural that independence would bring wide-ranging changes in the country's polity. The humiliation and restrictions faced by the Indians receded into the background because the grievances of the Africans were much greater and the need to reverse that discrimination more overpowering. The Indians were relatively better off in a poor society and the Africans saw the Asian community as one that had prospered during colonial rule.

Indians tried to recreate little Indias in African towns, with a more modern and affluent version of the locality back home. They remained Indians at heart in their daily lifestyle, rituals, manners, food and outlook. They congregated in Nairobi, where they were visible as a significant minority. There was frequent movement between India and Africa. Indians went to visit family homes and relatives, to study, for business and to get married. It meant much closer ties with the home family. Gujaratis, who formed 80 per cent of the Indian community, retained close contacts with the extended family in India, which provided them a ready crop of assistants and associates when required.

During the early years when Indians struggled for equality, they tended to ignore the Africans and their struggle against discrimination and exploitation. In this way, they cut themselves off from the Africans. The labour movement was the only area where the two ethnic groups came together to fight for their rights. Many Indians remained aloof, in spirit and culture, from their host societies. The cultural aloofness of the Indians made it easier to paint them as arrogant. In the initial years of political awakening in the African countries the majority of the Indian community chose to keep themselves apart, excluding themselves from the political arena where crucial decisions were taking place. Most of them did not identify with the new African nation in the making, for they believed themselves to be temporary residents.

The violent Mau Mau movement in Kenya was not directly targeted at the Asians but it unnerved the rich Asians. The Kenyan Indian Congress was vacillating, at times self-centred and generally uninvolved in African affairs. In the run-up to independence, the Kenyan National Congress voted to retain the communal roll, something that it had opposed for several decades. As independence drew closer, Indians began transferring funds overseas creating a lot of bad blood in the ruling circles of the new nation.

Indians were most reluctant to register for Kenyan citizenship; the majority preferred to retain their British passports. In Tanganiyika, now Tanzania, where Ismaili Khojas formed a substantial part of the Asian community, the Aga Khan directed his followers to adopt to African ways—to wear western clothes and make English and Swahili the medium of instruction in their schools. The official advice of the Indian government was that Indians should take the citizenship of the country of domicile if they planned to stay on in Africa. Prime Minister Jawaharlal Nehru pointed to the rising nationalism in the African states and called on the Indians to make common cause with the Africans. He specifically warned them not to look towards India for protection. But the Indians in Africa seemed unaware of the changing trends, and continued to live as though the world was not changing around them.

Relative affluence, a vulgar display of conspicuous consumption and a deep-rooted sense of cultural superiority have been the more visible attributes of a small section of the Indian elite in African countries. Though the majority of the Indian community were hardworking, simple people trying to make a living, the prosperity of the rich Indian businessman set the prevalent image for the Indian community as a whole. The White settlers, on the other hand, were quicker to change their behaviour towards the Africans as times changed, appointing Africans in highly visible positions in their enterprises and making them part of their social activities. This was in sharp contrast to the Indian family owned businesses and shops that relied on relatives to run their operations while their owners socialised in exclusive gatherings in their own community circles. It aggravated the underlying resentment among the Africans that had been fostered during the colonial days.

The first flush of nationalism brought increasing chauvinism;

Kenya for the Kenyans became the popular slogan. A policy of rapid Africanisation was began, with forced retirement of non-African personnel from railway and government jobs. Trading licenses coming up for renewal were transferred to Africans and some African leaders made public statements that the Indians were welcome to pack up and leave. Gradually more than half the Indian population left Kenya as the affirmative action policies cut down the jobs, and business opportunities for the Indian community dwindled.

The British Parliament had passed the Commonwealth Immigration Act in 1968 restricting the entry of Asian British passport holders into the country under a phased entry programme. It allowed entry to only those who could show evidence that a parent or a grandparent had been born in Britain. The increasingly strident public demands by Kenyan leaders that Asians should leave the country forced an exodus from Kenya. The Indian government made it clear that its responsibility related only to persons holding Indian passports. Those holding Kenyan or British citizenship were the responsibility of the respective governments. However, the government in New Delhi privately urged the Kenyan government to be fair in its dealing with the people of Indian origin in the country. At the same time the India government offered visas to all Asian British passport holders to stay in India while waiting for permission to enter Britain.

It was the means used for the Africanisation process that caused the maximum heartburn among the Asians. It showed that all non-citizens would have to eventually leave the country as Africans took over their jobs. Uganda hastened the process by adopting two laws in 1969, the Immigration Act and the Trade Licensing Act, which meant that all non-citizens had to reapply for resident permits within six months. The government got the opportunity to review the permits of all non-citizens and decide on who should be given a fresh resident permit. Under the Trade Licensing Act, the government designated areas where only African nationals could trade and also listed specific commodities that could only be traded by Africans.

In 1971 the Ugandan dictator, Idi Amin seized power in a coup and consolidated his position by murdering all perceived and potential opponents. In August 1972 while addressing the army, Idi Amin revealed that God had told him to order all Asians to quit Uganda. He accused the 80,000 Asian British passport holders of "sabotaging Uganda's economy and encouraging corruption". All Asians in Uganda had to submit proof of their Ugandan citizenship and several had their citizenship status summarily cancelled during scrutiny. As the exodus of Asians began, the economic effect of throwing them out became evident, for prices of property crashed, and the banks faced large-scale withdrawal of funds by the Asians. By the end of the month, it was decreed that the Asians could take only 50 pounds per head out of the country. Indian homes, properties, businesses were confiscated while security men looted the personal belongings of the Indians on their way to Kampala airport. Many Asians were left destitute, arriving in London with barely the clothes on their backs.

Idi Amin needed money, the economy was not in good shape and he had to pay the army that had backed him during the coup the year before. But the Ugandan dictator's brainwave did not bring him much cheer for the Indians departure resulted in an economic collapse. His methods were grotesque and severely damaged the country's economy, but they struck a chord in the African mind. The African prejudices against the Indians had been fostered and reinforced in the British run schools. The Indian traders were stereotyped as artful hoarders, who overcharged and fudged their accounts.

Idi Amin died on August 17, 2003 after 24 years in comfortable exile in Saudi Arabia. It took Uganda many years to recover from Idi Amin's rule. Aside from leading his country into economic collapse, he famously declared himself king of Scotland, enjoyed taunting world leaders while his men butchered thousands of Ugandans. Victorious rebel troops entering the dictator's palaces in 1979 found piles of corpses stored in some of the rooms.

The call for indigenisation has been and will continue to be raised in many parts of the world. Throwing the Asians out was a grand gesture, but Uganda has had to appeal to the Asians to return, President Yoweri Museveni urged the Asians to return and Indians are now a significant force in the economy once again. Not only have the Indians returned to Uganda, they have brought in investments worth about $1 billion into the Ugandan economy. A Departed Asians Property Custodian Board was set up to look at claims filed by returning Asians regarding their seized property. The Board has returned about 3490 properties to their owners, but getting repossession of the properties is a more complicated process.

There are about one-lakh persons of Indian origin living in Kenya and about 80,000 resident in Tanzania. Uganda has around 14,000 persons of Indian origin. About 16,000 people of Indian descent now live in Zimbabwe, most of them having moved to Zimbabwe from the other African countries. Asians who fled Uganda to settle in Britain and the US have prospered in the past two decades.

Chapter 8

Recent Migrants

The first Indians to reach Britain and North America were the sailors on the sailing ships that plied to India. The ships recruited Indians to replace sailors who had died during the voyages, and some Indian sailors jumped ship and disappeared into the local life in the port towns. The regular flow of immigrants began in the 20th century. There are now almost two million Indians living in the United States of America and about 1.2 million in Britain. The Indian community has come to be recognised as one of the most successful and prosperous ethnic minority in these countries. It is their success stories that are celebrated by the media in India and it is the Indian Americans who wield the most influence in political circles back in India.

The initial migration to North America was from Punjab, of ex-servicemen who had served overseas with the British forces in places like Hong Kong etc. A few of them reached Canada and as the accounts of the opportunities in this vast country spread, more Indians migrated to Canada. Some of them later moved down the West Coast to California. The mood in America was hostile to the immigrants from Asia, to the Chinese, Koreans and Japanese. Indians were late-comers to North America and formed a very small group but the early migrants faced hostility and discrimination since they were willing to work for lower wages.

Recruitment into the army was an important factor in maintaining prosperity in Punjab. The British land tenure system favoured the large landholders while small peasants were forced to mortgage their land in times of adversity to pay land revenues. Land was increasingly forfeited to the moneylenders. The army provided a source of income to the young villagers and after completing their service, many of them chose to look for work in different countries. Later migration itself opened another avenue and younger sons were encouraged to leave home and go abroad to work. The migrants were mostly Sikhs from four or five districts of Punjab, around Amritsar and Lahore.

From the villages of Punjab, small groups of men would set off for foreign lands. They sent for young nephews and cousins to join them on the journey. Most went with the blessings of their families for in these young men lay the families' hopes for a regular remittance. Land was mortgaged or sold to finance the journey in the expectation that the remittances would help buy back land and add to the family landholding. They travelled from Punjab to Calcutta by train and then took a ship to Hong Kong. There they stayed in the gurdwaras till they could board a ship to Vancouver, the main port on the Pacific Coast.

Chinese and Japanese migrants were the first Asians to reach Canada, and went to work on building the Canadian Pacific Railway, the rail link which connected the Atlantic and Pacific seaboards. Indians were late arrivals and found jobs on the railway, clearing land and logging, in farming and dairy work and fruit picking. In 1907 there were more than 2500 Indian immigrants in British Colombia.

Life was not easy for the early migrants because of economic and social discrimination. Organised European labour along the Pacific Coast wanted Asian workers excluded as "undesirable migrants." Canada was meant to be a White dominion settled by migrants from Britain and a few European countries. There were strong anti-Asian feelings among the European settlers against the influx of migrants from Japan and China. The hostility got directed against the Indians as well, but the demands to deport them were not followed through for fear of the adverse reaction in Punjab. The Indian immigrants were forced to live outside town in makeshift houses.

Immigration from Asia was actively discouraged; the Chinese Immigration Act specifically banned Chinese immigration while the Japanese government restricted migration to Canada under a gentleman's agreement with Canada. But there was no specific reference against Indians in the regulations. As British subjects Indians could not be barred from Canada but various methods were used to exclude Indians immigrants. In 1908 the Dominion government in Canada passed an order banning the entry of individuals who did not arrive in Canada by a "continuous journey" from their homeland. It effectively barred Indians for there was no direct shipping between India and Canada.

The harsh conditions in British Colombia brought the Indians together and the gurdwaras became a focal point of community life for them. The Indian workers set up the *Khalsa Diwan Society* to fight for the right to bring their families to Canada. In May 1914, several hundred Indians reached Vancouver on the *Komagata Maru*, a chartered ship that sought to bypass the continuous journey clause. The captain was ordered to anchor in the harbour and negotiations went on for two months as food stocks ran low. When the ship was ordered to sail off on July 18, the passengers mutinied and repulsed any attempt to board the ship. The episode ended with the ship being provisioned before it sailed out of Vancouver with its passengers.

Some Indians travelled down from Canada to California and found work in the construction of the Western Pacific Railway. As more Indians arrived, they took to working on the farms and orchards. Some of them moved into tenant farming, but they faced discrimination in the towns. There was strong hostility among the Anglo-Europeans towards the Asiatic immigrants. California was embroiled in militant anti-Asian immigrant politics with the Asian Exclusion League spearheading the campaign to keep out non-European immigrants. Even though there were only a few thousand Indians in California as the latest arrivals they bore the brunt of the animosity. Sikhs were called "rag-heads" by the exclusionist brigade, who hounded and harassed the Indian workers. The Indian community in California remained on the margins of society, but through hard work they were able to lease land for farming.

In 1910 a federal court had held in the US vs Balsara case that Indians, as descendants of Aryans were Caucasian. This meant that Indians could not be placed in the same restricted immigration category as the Chinese and the Japanese, who were listed as non-Caucasians race. In 1913 the Alien Land Act restricted the ownership of land to American citizens or those eligible for grant of citizenship. The federal Immigration Act of 1917 listed India in its 'Asian barred zone' that barred immigration from those countries.

In 1923, the US Supreme Court overturned the Balsara ruling in the US vs Thind case. The court held that Bhagat Singh Thind was not White in colour or in culture and therefore could not be granted citizenship. As a result of the judgement the US immigration authorities began cancelling the citizenship granted to Indians. In California where the majority of the Indians lived, their land titles were cancelled under the Alien Land Act. It meant that Indians who had bought land had to transfer it to the names of their wives, if they were eligible for citizenship or their America born children or even to friends to escape forfeiture of their land.

There were two groups of Indians in the United States, the

workers and farmers in California and a growing number of Indian students on the East Coast. In 1923 Lala Har Dayal began publishing the *Ghadar* newspaper with money raised by Indian workers. The paper was a means of communication among the Indians and to propagate the call for India's independence. When World War I began in 1914 many Indians returned home to stage an uprising against British rule. The ship, *Tosa Maru* carrying *Ghadarites* to India was detained at Calcutta port and over a hundred men were interned under the wartime regulations.

The anti-Asian perception in America began to change with World War II when India, China and the Philippines were on the side of the Allied forces. Asian organisations in the US lobbied with the government to change the immigration laws and in 1946 the Filipino Naturalisation Act did away with the Asian barred zone concept, setting immigration quotas (105 for Indians) from individual Asian countries.

Despite the hardships and restrictions, America was still a land of opportunity for the migrants. Dilip Singh Saund who had migrated in 1920 was granted citizenship in 1949, three years after the change in regulations. Saund was elected to the House of Representatives from California in 1956 and was re-elected in 1958 but did not complete his second term due to ill health. He is still the only Indian to be elected to the US Congress.

A major change in the immigration policy occurred with the 1965 amendments to the Immigration and Nationality Act. The need for skilled labour, the increasing number of wives of US servicemen joining their husbands from Korea and Japan brought about the changes. It removed discrimination based on country of origin and established three criteria for prospective migrants: occupational skills needed in the US, family re-unification and political or religious refugees. Indians became one of the main beneficiaries of the change. Indian immigration to the US began as a trickle in the late 1960s, but just over two decades later the

Indian community had become the largest Asian group after the Chinese and Filipinos in the country.

Like the United States and Canada, Australia and New Zealand were also considered new lands reserved for White settlement. These countries welcomed migrants from European countries while keeping out migrants from Japan and China. Racial exclusion implied that the alien race was inferior in its cultural attributes and characteristics and therefore had to be kept out. One of the reasons offered for excluding Asian migrants was that it was necessary to protect the rights and interests of the white work force. The other was the difficulty for Asians in assimilating in the new society.

Overpopulation and the shortage of resources in the European countries were overcome by substantial migration to the New World countries. But the Asian countries and peoples, facing similar problems of overpopulation, were barred from these sparsely populated, resource rich territories. In the early 1900s, Japan took the position that racial equity was an important factor linked to the principle of equity among nations. The major push against the Asian exclusionist policies came from the Japanese and Chinese governments. Japanese anger had been fuelled by the '*Whites only*' immigration in the post-World War I years, since Japan considered that its growing population had the natural territorial right to settle in Oceania. Japanese immigration was one of the central problems in US-Japanese relations before World War II. Japan saw it as a territorial dispute while China, on the other hand, saw the exclusion policy as one of racial discrimination.

During World War II, China's resistance against the Japanese onslaught became critically import to the Allied powers in the Pacific theatre. It tied down the main part of the Japanese armed forces in China, giving respite to the American forces. By 1942, the Chinese leaders were demanding an end to Chinese exclusion policies, making it a test of friendship. The demands found an echo in the United States as well and in 1943 the Chinese exclusion policy ended with a small annual quota allotted for Chinese migrants. Canada followed suit. Open racial discrimination and the concept of superiority of races had become anathema after the experience of Nazism in Europe.

The immigration restrictions in the British Dominions became a major obstruction during the debate in India over remaining a part of the Commonwealth after independence. The United States had allowed a token Indian immigration in 1946 but the Dominions continued with their discriminatory policies. Indian leaders warned that India could not stay as a member of the Commonwealth if Indians were not free to enter parts of it. The exclusive immigration policies became a matter of principle in Asian countries for racial equity and non-discrimination. Though America and Canada dropped the exclusion regulations, the discrimination continued in the number of Asians allowed entry as compared to European migrants.

America found that as the leader of the free world, having race-based discriminatory policies was a major disadvantage during the Cold War years. It gave the Soviet Union the means to paint the United States as racist and discriminatory in its policies throughout the Asian region. It was a damaging image at a time when the two superpowers were jockeying for influence over Asia. The pernicious effect of the exclusionist immigration policies became more evident in foreign relations, but opposition in the US Congress held up the new laws. The Civil Rights movement in the United States brought a change in the mood in the country against all blatant forms of discrimination. A sustained campaign of lobbying by immigrant groups helped change attitudes among the lawmakers. The 1967 amendments to the law finally removed all barriers base on race.

Canada followed a similar path, but its reasons for dropping its '*White Canada*' policy were even more urgent. A Canadian Foreign Office assessment indicated that the restrictive immigration policy had affected the growth of friendly relations with China, Japan, India, Pakistan and Sri Lanka. The formation of the United Nations Organisation had made social values and civil rights a new factor in international relations. UN members had accepted the obligation to eliminate racial discrimination. The International Labour Organisation also provided a platform for Asian countries to attack the discriminatory immigration policies. Without significant military and economic power, Canada nonetheless looked for a prominent position in international affairs. For enhanced prestige and importance in the international arena, Canada had to gain influence and make new friends and allies. But it could not do so with the tag of racial bias at a time when the decolonisation process was creating a number of new states.

The 1950s was a period of extraordinary warmth in bilateral ties because of the personal equation between Indian and Canadian leaders. Canada was a significant aid donor in the 1950s, giving up to Canadian $100 million annually in the 1960s. In 1951 Canada allowed a small quota for immigrants from India, Pakistan and Sri Lanka. It helped to dilute the charge of racial discrimination against Canada. The migrants were chosen on the ability to adjust to life in Canada, which meant only urban, well-qualified individuals passed muster. In 1957, India's quota was raised to 300, while close relatives of Canadian citizens could enter as non-quota migrants.

In 1956 the Canadian government dropped race as a criterion in its immigration policy and the revised regulations in 1967 removed the in-built advantage for European migrants by instituting a points system based on skills in demand in Canada. Twenty years later Canada accepted its cultural diversity as an important feature of Canada's identity.

The Indian community in Canada is now largely urban centred in Toronto, Vancouver, Montreal, Edmonton and Calgary. Unlike the Indian community in the United States, in Canada the community is a mixed one with both highly qualified professionals and semi-skilled, rural migrants. This is mainly due to the family sponsorship immigration policy in Canada. The chain migrations through blood and marital bonds current kept the links with the home base and also helped retain a kinship structure that corresponds to the life in the village in Punjab. The kinship support also ensured that the migrants concentrated in some regions of Canada, which had added to their political importance.

Ujjal Dossanjh of the New Democratic Party, who migrated to Canada in 1968, became the first person of Indian descent to be elected Premier of British Columbia Province. Indo-Canadians are becoming increasingly politically conscious. Mainstream Canadian political parties actively woo the Canadian Indian community. An annual Baisakhi function is held in the Canadian Parliamentary complex and is attended by the Prime Minister and Cabinet Ministers. There are half a dozen Indian Canadians in Parliament.

Indians had gone to Australia in the 19th Century as camel handlers when Australia introduced camels in the country. Some of the camel drovers stayed on after their three-year contact was over. Later a few Indians arrived as cane cutters and traders. But the Immigration Act of 1901 stopped all immigration from India. Even as the United States and Canada changed their immigration regulations, Australia was going strong with its '*White Australia*' policy, arguing that immigration was a domestic issue. It generated a good deal of ill feeling in Asia with its defence of its policy. Australia took much longer to realise that as a country located in Asia it could not continue with discriminatory policies that were considered repugnant throughout the world. The '*White Australia*' policy that so infuriated Asians was finally buried in 1973.

New Zealand was not ready to go the Australian way of disregarding world opinion and defending racially biased policies. New Zealand also considered itself as a country of European development, and it chose the means of unwritten regulations to bar Asian immigration. Asian applications were rejected without assigning any reasons. It saved New Zealand from the opprobrium of racial discrimination since it portrayed a picture of racial harmony between its White and Maori residents. New Zealand lost its assured market for agricultural products when Britian moved towards membership of the European Economic Community (EEC) and had to look for markets in Asia. In 1974 New Zealand ended the automatic entry granted to British nationals. But it took another four years before it removed race as a determining factor in its immigration policy. The National Party government of Robert Muldoon launched a campaign against Pacific Islanders who overstayed their short-term work permits. Police raids flushed out the overstayers to be deported, creating a furore in the South Pacific island territories. The campaign had an immediate and damaging effect on New Zealand's relations with its neighbours. In 1978 New Zealand adopted a non-discriminatory immigration policy.

The changes in immigration policies began as governments realised its implications in international relations, as Asian goodwill became a matter of considerable importance to fight the Communist threat in the region. International intolerance of racial discrimination increased as the battle against South Africa's apartheid policies gained strength.

While American and Canadian polices were being liberalised, Britain was becoming more restrictive in its procedures. In the post war decades Britain faced a labour shortage and was liberal in giving visas for workers. Britain began to restrict the entry of immigrants by the 1960s. South Asians came to Britain in the 1950s and early 1960s to take up work in the textile mills and other similar jobs. The initial influx was from Punjab, followed by Indians from the Caribbean and later from East Africa countries.

By 1962, Britain had tightened its immigration norms; ending the principle that all citizens of Commonwealth countries had free and unrestricted entry. Citizens of Canada, Australia and New

Zealand retained their right of entry, but the right of other Commonwealth citizens whose passports were not issued in the UK was curtailed. Migration was restricted to those who were able to obtain employment vouchers on the basis of a recognised skill or qualification that was in short supply in Britain. In the 1960s the majority of Indian migrants came in as dependants for the extended family system in Punjab villages provided ways to list nephews and cousins as dependants. Nephews became sons, cousins were brothers, and uncles were called '*bade papa*' (elder father). They came and found work in the textile and garment industry, in the steel industry, railways and bus companies.

The early migrants settled in London, Birmingham and Manchester. They settled in the inner cities near the workplaces and in Indian settlements. Most of the migrants intended to return home after earning enough for a comfortable life. They sought to retain their sense of identity and separateness from the local community and lived close together to recreate their rural culture. It tended to make them more visible as a distinct community with their alien customs. It was a despised and ignored minority but the community's success in Britain's multicultural society has wrought many changes over the decades. Indian cooking smells had bothered the British at one time, but in the 1990s chicken *tika masala* (spicy piece) had replaced fish and chips as the favourite British take-away food.

The population of Indian origin in Britain is a mixed one, comprising the different waves of migrations of the 1950s and 1960s, the East African Asians, the well-educated recent migrants and second generation Indians. The early migrants came as workers for lower end jobs but many of those arriving from East Africa brought with them trading and entrepreneurial skills and some capital. Uprooted from their homes, they were determined to rebuild their lives and their hard work changed the image of the Indian community in Britain within a couple of decades. In the

1970s they ran the small corner shops in British towns but 20 years later they had expanded to bigger enterprises, making the Indian community one of the most prosperous minority groups in the country. The strong Indians values of the family pooling its resources, both financial and human, have been an important factor in their entrepreneurial successes.

Indians have a sizeable presence in the British National Health Service, but statistics show that they rarely become consultants. First generation Indians were too busy settling in to take an interest in local politics, but second generation Indians are more confident in stepping into new areas. They are politically conscious and have begun taking an active part in political activity in the city council and local bodies. The Indian concentration in parts of London and other towns ensures that they are no longer ignored the main political parties. In the May 2002 elections three Members of Parliament of Indian origin were elected. Indians number among the list of British millionaires and they feature regularly in the New Year honours list. The Labour government elevated several Indians as peers in the House of Lords.

In the United States, the Indian population is considered among the most successful and wealthy immigrant communities. The Indians who came to America in the late 1960s and 1970s were highly qualified individuals. About 7000 Indians from Uganda were granted immigration under a special clause. Till the 1980s, the Indians were a professional class dispersed throughout the suburbs, living among other middleclass people. Later the family unification scheme allowed them to sponsor their kin for immigration. The newer arrivals moved into low paying jobs, as they did not have similar level of educational skills as the original migrants.

From the affluent professional and the millionaire IT entrepreneurs, the community stretches through middle level managers, hotel owners, retail shopkeepers to the low end wage earners like taxi drivers, salespersons and factory workers. They own more than 40 per cent of motels in America and 25 per cent of its smaller hotels. In recent years, they are finding a place in the corporate world; they are lawyers, academics, and journalists and are making a name for themselves in the creative arts. A good part of the community is well off with a fabulously wealthy elite that forms the popular image of the Indians living in the US and in Britain but the community is much more diverse. The glowing reports of individual success among the Indians have crowded out the sight of the poor among the community. A majority of the taxi drivers in New York are South Asian.

The majority of the Indian community is relatively new in America. About three-fourths of the community is below 45 years of age and it has the largest percentage of foreign born. As a community Indians have been slow to obtain American citizenship. Most Indians who went to America in the early years of migration did so for better educational and professional opportunities. Most of them planned to return after a Masters degree, a few years of work experience in America and making a bundle of money. In many cases, the return home did not take place for various reasons, including adaptation to a better life style, greater opportunities for advancement and professional satisfaction. But most Indian Americans retained their permanent resident status till their children began growing up. With no possibility of their children choosing to relocate to India, citizenship became an important issue within the Indian American community.

Indians were late in seeking the leverage of their economic power to gain political influence, despite the example of other immigrant groups in the US. A lack of unity among the large number of Indian groups, a general disinterest in civic and political affairs, and a preoccupation with making a success of their careers were the reasons for keeping away. It is issues pertaining to the community that usually stir Indian political activism. It was lobbying by the Association of Indians in America that finally led to the inclusion of the category of "Asian Indian" in the 1980 Census in America. About 3,60,000 Indians were listed in the 1980 Census and by the 1990s the Indian population had gone up to 1.6 million. There are a plethora of Indian organisations in the United States, many of them corresponding to different regions and communities in India. Indian organisations also have a penchant for splitting, with rival factions establishing their own set-ups. Rivals groups hold separate parades for Independence Day in New York.

The community took time to understand that they were unlikely to influence policy-making even when it had significant relevance to them without integrating completely in the American way of life. It meant getting actively involved in the political processes. Indians took their first step with political contributions. Wealthy doctors and other professionals began making contributions to individual candidates running for public office. However, the Indian tendency has been to aim at the top levels of politics, and contribute to fund-raisers for Senators and Congressmen. Second generation Indian Americans are American citizens by birth and have generally a stronger sense of civic and political responsibility, and have begun a more vigorous participation in American politics.

In America, as in Canada, Britain, Australia and New Zealand, the Indian population shows a wide diversity. There are significant differences between the migrants from India and those arriving from the former colonies. Indians from Trinidad, Guyana, South Africa, Kenya, Uganda, Tanzania and Fiji have been tempered by their sojourn in these countries. Indians form a diverse group in these countries, displaying a wide variety that reflects the diversity of India but also the different orientations of Indians who left the motherland a couple of generations ago. Within the broad structure of Indian heritage, there are many differences in their cultural outlook. They have maintained cultural values drawn from the traditional practices their grandparents took with them from India. These differences occasionally cause friction among the different groups.

There are large groups of Fiji Indians living in Australia and New Zealand, most of them left Fiji after the military coups in 1987 and 2000. Vancouver is the largest settlement of Fiji Indians outside Fiji. The Indians who have migrated to Australia from Fiji find that they are stricter in maintaining the old traditions and practices than the Indians from India. In New York Indians from the Caribbean find that their religious ceremonies bear little similarity with the rituals practiced by migrants from urban India. There has been friction between Fiji Indians and the migrants from India on many occasions; the Fiji Indians complain that the '*Indiawalas*' believe that they are the authentic Indians and all others are pale imitations.

After opening up to non-discriminatory immigration, the United States, Canada, Australia, Britain and New Zealand turned into multi-ethnic, multi-cultural societies over the years. From the melting pot style of assimilation that enforced conformity on its members, American society began to value its cultural diversity. Canada made a formal announcement of its multi-cultural ethos. Australia had a wider ethnic mix with Chinese, Japanese, Koreans, Vietnamese, Pacific Islanders and South Asians.

The melting pot metaphor dominated the American immigrant experience till the 1970s when the arrival of a large number of non-Caucasian immigrants brought a variety of cultural traditions. By the later decades a much more radical approach to ethnic diversity came into existence. The emphasis shifted to terms like kaleidoscope, salad bowl, and multi-cultural mosaic. Ethnicity is celebrated as the migrant imbibes American values. To retain a sense of ethnic identity has become acceptable and even encouraged among second-generation migrants. Indians have been major beneficiaries of the changing perceptions in these countries.

Chapter 9

In the Gulf Region

In the 1970s another region to India's west opened up to migrant workers. The Gulf region is part of India's extended neighbourhood with which it has had a regular mercantile interaction through the ages. Indian settlements have existed in the Gulf region for centuries and Indian goods were distributed throughout the region. The trade channels flourished through the colonial period when the Indian rupee was legal tender right up to the port of Aden. The oil boom of the 1970s changed the face of the countries in the Gulf region; flush with oil revenues to pay for grand developmental plans, these countries needed to import a labour force to execute the projects. The construction boom started regular labour migration to these countries, initially from the Arab countries and later from South Asia.

In the late 1970s, Indian skilled, semi-skilled and manual workers went to the Gulf countries through private recruitment agencies. A decade later, falling oil revenues reduced the jobs in the construction sector but more Indians found work in banking and other service sectors. The Gulf region is now the main destination of Indians going abroad to work. Over 3 million Indians live in the Gulf Cooperation Council (GCC) countries, in the United Arab Emirates, Saudi Arabia, Kuwait, Oman, Qatar and Bahrain. About 70 per cent of the Indians in the Gulf region are skilled and semi-skilled workers, about 20 per cent have white-collared jobs in offices as clerks, accountants and managers with another 10 per cent professionals and entrepreneurs.

As the Gulf countries have diversified into industrial and commercial activity, Indians have turned entrepreneurs, investing in retail stores, gold and textile trade, hotels, restaurants, IT companies and joint ventures. Indians have also become involved in business and industrial ventures in the UAE and other investment friendly economies in the region. The Free Zones promoted by the Gulf governments have provided an attractive environment for investment with no taxes, no restriction on foreign investment, and top class infrastructure.

The Persian Gulf is an important region for India; the GCC is India's second largest trading partner second only to America, the second largest importer of Indian goods and provides a major part of India's oil and gas imports. It is also the source of a large part of the remittances to India. The Indians in the Gulf countries fall in a different category from all other overseas Indians settled abroad. They are Indian expatriates, who are in the Gulf region on short-term work permits. Since the Gulf countries do not allow naturalisation, Indians residing in these countries do not have the option to stay on as migrant Indians have in western countries. There is a regular turnover in the Indian population in these countries; migrants return home on completing their term though some may return for a second or third term. The usual length of stay among working class migrants is between 5 – 8 years.

The majority of the Indians workers are relatively young males who travel alone to take up their jobs. Conditions in the work areas are strict and most workers live in camps in austere, dormitory style accommodation provided by their employers. The work permit specifies the name of the employer and no change of job is allowed, the workers have to leave the country if dismissed from their jobs. Only migrants earning a salary above a prescribed limit are allowed to take their families with them, but many of them do not as living costs are high and educational facilities are limited. The objective of most Indians working in the Gulf States is to save money for their return to India. Indians in the Gulf are purely temporary migrants and the majority of them send their savings back to India.

Unlike the Indians working in other countries, their savings rate is high since there are few avenues for spending money, especially since their immediate family resides in India. Migrants in the developed countries have a higher expenditure as their families usually accompany them. They also need to keep the major part of their savings in local banks and other monetary instruments, and remit only a small part of their savings to India.

Indians are the largest expatriate community in several countries such as Saudi Arabia, UAE, Bahrain, Oman and Qatar. There are about 15 lakh Indians in Saudi Arabia, 9 lakhs in the UAE, 2.8 lakhs in Kuwait, 3.4 lakhs in Oman, 1.3 lakhs in Bahrain and 1.25 lakhs in Qatar according to the report of the High Level Committee on the Indian Diaspora. The number of Indian expatriates in Kuwait and Saudi Arabia increased after the Gulf War in 1991 when the Kuwaiti and Saudi authorities tightened their entry procedures to restrict the entry of Palestinian and Yemeni workers. Indians are valued in the Gulf region as a disciplined, hard working work force that does not involve itself in local matters. Saudi authorities approved the employment of Indians as they were well qualified and unlike the Arabs did not bring new cultural influences into the local society. The Gulf countries are essentially work areas for overseas workers for limited periods and the Arab governments keep social contact between the local Arabs and the migrant workers to a minimal level to avoid any new cultural and social influences on the local population.

In the early decades of the Gulf rush there were widespread complaints about mistreatment and underpayment by employers as well as misrepresentation and fraud by recruiting agencies. The Arab states do not allow any trade union activity and there was considerable hardship for workers who were at odds with their employers or sponsors, especially as employers retained custody of the workers passports and other legal documents. Many workers did not know the exact terms and conditions of their contracts nor did they have any means of redressal for breach of contract by the employer.

Indians went out as carpenters, welders, masons, electricians, fitters, helpers; most of them did not fully understand the conditions of work. Many found themselves relegated to manual work even if they were hired as skilled workers. There were disputes over delayed or non-payment of salaries for months, denial of annual leave for long periods and other conditions specified in the contract. The semi-literate workers seldom had any recompense against their employers, especially when the company defaulted or went bankrupt.

Reports of ill treatment and defrauding of workers led to a number of cases being filed in Indian courts. In 1979 the Supreme Court handed down guidelines for emigration regulations till fresh legislation was enacted. The Emigration Act of 1983 incorporated the guidelines and provided a regulatory framework with appropriate safeguards for migrating workers. Under the 1983 Act all recruiting agencies had to be registered with the Union Ministry of Labour after presenting satisfactory evidence of their bonafides and financial soundness, experience in handling manpower export and producing a bank guarantee ranging between Rs 3 lakhs to Rs 10 lakhs depending on the scale of operations. The security deposit was meant to meet contingencies such as workers being stranded by their employers and for sending back bodies of deceased workers. In 2004 there were about 1377 registered recruiting agencies including nine state manpower export corporations.

Under the regulations, workers required clearance from the Protector of Emigrants before going abroad. The recruiting agent has to provide a copy of the letter from the prospective employer specifying his requirement, a power of attorney from the employer to the recruiting agent and a copy of the work contract with the service conditions to obtain the clearance. The documents have to be accompanied by an affidavit from the agent authenticating the documents. Individuals applying for clearance need to produce passports stamped with an employment visa and a copy of the work contract.

As the demand for Indian workers increased, the government prepared a model employment contract that set out the terms and conditions of employment as a safeguard for the Indian emigrants. The standardised agreement was revised from time to time to incorporate changes in work conditions. Over the years there has been a progressive liberalisation of the emigration policy by increasing the number of categories of persons who do not require emigration clearance before taking up jobs abroad. It has resulted in a sharp increase in the number of workers going abroad.

Work conditions have improved in the last decade with the increasing number of Indians living in the Gulf countries. The adverse publicity from instances of ill treatment and exploitation has led to local authorities strengthening the grievance settlement procedures. In the early days of the labour influx in the Gulf, the local authorities often ignored protests in the belief that no labour exporting country would make a strong intervention on behalf of their workers. The changing international mood regarding human rights of individuals, democratic freedoms and legal rights of migrant workers has influenced the attitude of governments in the region, with more effective grievance redressal mechanisms in place.

In the year 2003, 4.66 lakh workers immigrated for employment to countries in the Gulf, Malaysia and Singapore. The major component was from Kerala at 92,044 workers, 89,464 from Tamil Nadu, 65,971 from Andhra Pradesh and 37,693 from Rajasthan, according to Labour Ministry statistics. Remittances in 2002-2003 were to the tune of $14.8 billion. With the large number of young men going to the Gulf to work, the remittance economy became a major factor in Kerala's economy.

A study by the Centre for Development Studies on Kerala's Gulf Connection: Emigration, Remittances and their Economic Impact (1972-2000) showed that remittances formed 22 per cent of the State's income in the late nineties. By the end of the 1990s, they were higher than the State expenditure, and also higher than the value addition in the manufacturing and industrial sector. There are an estimated 13.62 lakh people from Kerala working abroad, which is almost ten per cent of the total workforce of the State. Remittances have made significant changes in the consumption patterns in the state, from white goods to construction material for new houses, lavish spending on festivals and marriages. But it has led to little industrial activity since the majority of the migrants were skilled and unskilled workers and their remittances have been mainly used to meet the living expenses of their families back home.

Remittances from the Gulf region form over 40 per cent of the inward remittances into India. Remittances have risen in the past few years as the expatriates have shifted from the informal channels of sending money home to the regular money transfers through banks and other money changing organisations. The international efforts to tighten up money transfers to curb money laundering after the terrorist attacks in America has made it more risky to use the informal market 'hundi' or 'hawala' route. Advertisements and offices of agents of Western Union and other money transfer companies dot the countryside in Kerala and Punjab.

Saudi Arabia and the UAE have a large floating population of illegal migrants. The easy sailing from the Indian coast to the UAE makes it relatively easy for the transport of illegal workers to the Gulf on dhows or country craft, which are also used for smuggling of gold, silver and other contraband. Some Indians entering Saudi Arabia for the Haj pilgrimage have stayed back to look for work as illegal residents. Any worker who leaves his employer, whether due to harassment or any other reason becomes an illegal resident. They manage to find work but live in fear of exposure and at the mercy of unscrupulous employers. Illegal migrants are unable to leave the country for lack of proper documents. Some illegal migrants take to begging, while others have been involved in smuggling, extortion and petty crime. The UAE and Saudi authorities have periodically held an amnesty to allow the illegal migrants to leave the country on temporary permits. The UAE government declared a four-month long amnesty for illegal immigrants from January 1, 2003 and issued about 24,243 emergency exit certificates to illegal Indian immigrants to let them return home.

Private recruiters and travel agents continue to send young Indians to the Gulf region, charging them large sums as commissions without adequate arrangements or protection. Those desperate to find jobs abroad find ways to circumvent the regulations, and sometimes the desperation of the job seekers themselves leads them to fall prey to job rackets and the false promises of agents.

In June 2004 the Indian government intervened to arrange the release and repatriation of three Indians working at an American army camp in Iraq. Peter Thomas of Mavelikkara in Kerala related his experience in an interview to Indian newspapers. Thomas and his two associates worked in the laundry and did odd jobs in the American camp, where they were treated worse than animals, he said. They were employed by Dawood and Partner, a Jordanian company, who were subcontractors to an American Company, Kellogg, Brown and Root. The Indian workers were not paid their full wages, their conditions were miserable and they could not leave as their passports were in the custody of their employers. They were told that they would be working in Jordan, but were sent off to Iraq. It was with great difficulty that they could make contact the Indian mission and find their way home.

A spate of newspaper reports on the attempts of private manpower agencies to hire former army personnel to work as support staff to the American forces in Iraq forced the Indian government to ban the recruitment. The Indian government suspended the grant of clearances for Indian workers to go to Iraq on April 25, 2004. Three weeks later the ban was extended to Kuwait, Jordan and the UAE as these countries had become the route to take workers to Iraq.

The Washington Post of July 1 described the experience of D Ayajakumar of Kollam in Kerala, who was recruited for a job in Kuwait by a Mumbai based employment agency, Subhash Vijay Associates. He paid Rs 80,000 for a job with Gulf Catering Co of Riyadh. The Saudi company was a subcontractor to Alargan Group of Kuwait, which in turn was a subcontractor to Event Services of Salt Lake City that had a subcontract from KBR of Houston. Ajayakumar was among several Indians hired for jobs in Kuwait, Saudi Arabia, and Jordan and then transferred to Iraq against their will.

Three Indians, Antaryami, Tilak Raj and Sukhdev were among a group of seven truck drivers taken hostage in Iraq and released after protracted negotiations. The militant group that held them hostage threatened to behead them unless their employers, the Kuwait Gulf Link Company withdrew its operations from Iraq and paid compensation for American inflicted damage in Falluja. On their return to India, the three Indians revealed that they had been sent to Kuwait by the Mumbai based Om Sai Travels and had travelled on a three-month visitors visa after seeking suspension of emigration clearance to visit relatives. They were driving cargo trucks in Iraq when they were taken hostage.

Workers in the Gulf region become vulnerable and at the mercy of their employers who keep their passports in their custody. Local employers in league with recruitment agencies in India run a system in which employers obtain extra employment visas and then send the "extra" workers out to work for other employers after taking a cut from their monthly salaries. Most of the poor workers are too timid or unsure of the remedy available to them to get out of the situation they find themselves in. Indian workers who have taken huge loans to finance the overseas employment are forced into those work conditions in order to repay their loans.

At the time of the hostage crisis in Iraq, the Labour Ministry had estimated that there were 5024 Indians were in Iraq. Most of them did not have visas for Iraq and despite the Indian embassy's suggestion to leave Iraq because of the unsafe conditions; few of them were willing to leave their employment.

The category of domestic workers is among the most vulnerable section of workers in the Gulf region. The labour laws of these countries do not cover domestic workers, or those who work inside homes. While skilled and semi-skilled workers living in camps have the solace of being in the company of friends and relatives, it is the domestic workers who are likely to face exploitative situations in their work place because of their employers' attitude towards servants. Working in the close confines of a house, domestic workers have been treated with disdain and even contempt by their employers. A large number of Indians in Kuwait are domestic workers, employed as cooks, drivers, guards, gardeners, housemaids and governesses.

In 2001 the Indian government prohibited the emigration of women below the age of 30 years for jobs as housemaids. Women from Philippines and Indonesia now dominate this kind of domestic work, but Indian women also manage to evade the government ban by travelling through Nepal or other routes. Individuals can seek 'suspension' of the requirement of emigration clearance by stating that they are travelling on vacation or going to visit relatives.

In 2003 the National Human Rights Commission took up the case of a woman domestic worker from Andhra Pradesh who had committed suicide in Saudi Arabia. The father, who lived in a small town in India, was informed that the body was being kept in the mortuary and was asked to pay for the transportation of the body of the deceased woman to India. The employer of the poor woman had disclaimed any obligation in the matter. The family of the deceased woman contacted the NHRC through some social activists. The NHRC wrote to the Ministry of External Affairs to take it up the issue of salary and compensation with the Saudi authorities and make arrangements for sending the body to India.

Indians holding professional and middle-income service sector jobs constitute a substantial number of the over 3 million Indians in the Gulf countries. The large Indian community in the Gulf region has resulted in the sprouting of a number of Indian associations of various hues. Some of the associations have taken up the cases of Indian workers with local authorities and the Indian missions. Many of them have articulated the demands and concerns of different sections of the Indian expatriates in the Gulf countries.

The needs and requirements of Indians in the Gulf are quite different to other overseas Indians. They are directly affected by Indian government policies. Since they return home after their contract term ends, they seek special concessions in customs duties to facilitate their return to India and repatriate their funds home.

The community associations have a long list of grievances and requests directed to the Indian government. They complain that though the Indians in the Gulf are the section that has regularly sent the largest amount of remittances to India, they are ignored in the government's efforts to woo overseas Indians. The government's concentration on the Indian diaspora in the west has meant that their interests do not get the attention they deserve.

Among their demands is reserving two nominated seats in the Rajya Sabha for NRIs and providing voting rights, which allow them to vote in the Indian elections. However, some of their problems and requests relate to procedural delays and streamlining certain facilities, while others pertain to providing relief and assistance to workers.

The NRIs in the Gulf keep their money in India and many of them have faced difficulties in their financial dealings in India for the lack of adequate safeguards. There are complaints about fraud by overseas branches of Indian banks, uncaring and careless dealing by bank employees in their hometown. Fixed deposit receipts from NRI accounts are misplaced, and debentures and bond certificates are frequently not sent to the forwarding addresses. Dividend warrants and fixed deposits have been fraudulently encashed, sometimes with the connivance of bank staff through fake power of attorney documents. NRIs find it difficult to evict tenants from their properties when they return home. Affluent NRIs in the Gulf are now looking at new avenues for investment, which can range from the Indian equity markets, the mutual funds and real estate for investment purposes that would give better returns than fixed deposits. But procedural problems in applying for shares and delayed payments have acted as a deterrent for many prospective investors.

Education for their children has continued to exercise the NRIs in the Gulf. The limited opportunities for higher education means that children have to be sent back to India to study. Many of them face problems getting admission to colleges of their choice because of state government regulations requiring three-year continuous domicile in the state for admission to the majority of the seats in educational institutions. The government allowed all educational institutions to set aside a 15 per cent quota for wards of non-resident Indians with a higher fee structure. Early in 2004, the government took the decision to institute a special quota for the Gulf NRIs. The All India Council for Technical Education (AICTE) issued a notification that one-third of the 15 per cent supernumerary seats in educational institutions offering technical courses would be reserved for NRIs in the Gulf region. It decreed that the tuition fees for the NRIs from the Gulf region would be at par with other Indians students, thereby removing a major cause of complaint among the NRIs in the Gulf countries.

Indians in the Gulf have often protested at the high airfares charged on the Gulf sector. NRIs contend that it costs almost the same to fly from the Gulf to the US as it does to reach Calicut, which is one-third of the distance. Indian air carriers have tried to explain that airfares depend on a variety of factors that include IATA regulatory fare structures, seasonal demand and off-season discounts. The demand for lower airfares got stronger after a Gulf budget airline; the Sharjah based Air Arabia revealed plans to fly to Kerala at half the normal fare. A few Indian associations in the Gulf had even given a call to boycott Air India flights in March 2004. Air India has since announced its intention to start a 'no-frills' air carrier to cater to the Gulf sector, beginning April 2005.

At an interface between the Kerala state government, Ministry of External Affairs and NRI organisations held in July 2004, the NRIs asked for more Malayali speaking officials to be posted at the Indian diplomatic missions because of the large number of workers from Kerala. The External Affairs Ministry agreed to set up a round-the-clock telephone based helpline at the missions to provide advice and guidance to Indians in the region. They asked for a simplified procedure for verification of educational certificates in India. After the UAE authorities discovered several instances of forged Indian certificates, all educational certificates are required to be certified by the diplomatic missions at the time of granting work visas. The certification is done on the basis of verification and attestation by the Ministry of Human Resource Development and the External Affairs Ministry, which leads to delays.

On December 25, 2003 the government notified the Pravasi Bharatiya Yojana, a mandatory insurance scheme for all workers seeking emigration clearance. The scheme is being implemented by six insurance companies who provide an insurance cover of Rs 2 lakhs for a period of two years against death or permanent disability. It also covers medical treatment in India for the worker to the tune of Rs 50,000. In case of death, it provides for the transportation of the dead body to India and a one-way ticket for one attendant. In case the worker is stranded because the employer does not receive him on arrival, or makes substantive changes in the work conditions or sacks him within three months of arrival, the worker is entitled to reimbursement of one-way airfare to his hometown.

An Emigration Amendment bill was introduced in Parliament in November 2002, but the bill lapsed when the Lok Sabha was dissolved before the general elections. The proposed legislation had included provision for setting up a Manpower Export Promotion Council, which would study the needs, demands and condition of the international labour market around the world to give information to prospective emigrants. Prospective emigrants to the Gulf countries require proper counselling and orientation in order to enhance their ability to adapt to new work and social conditions and also compete with migrants from other countries.

Chapter 10

Dual Citizenship

The majority of first generation migrants who went to the United States and Britain saw themselves as sojourners, going west to make their careers with every intention of coming back home after a few years. This is the reason why the Indian rate of naturalisation in the US is low compared to other immigrant groups. Most Indians preferred to retain permanent resident status as Green card holders. They were economic migrants so the desire to return was kept alive, even when it became a distant dream. The first generation migrants were not cut off from their homes like the indentured immigrants. Their migration was voluntary. For most of them, migration was an entrepreneurial exercise, obviously so, in the case of the Gujarati traders and also for the Punjabi peasant whose travel expenses were funded by the joint family for eventual betterment of its fortunes. The migrants came, not from the poorest strata, but were those who could afford to raise the money to travel abroad. Those going as students or for professional jobs had homes and families to tie them to the homeland. Their migration was meant to be a limited sojourn for economic prosperity and then return home to a life of comfort.

As the years went by, when their children began growing up in the foreign lands, the idea of return was pushed off to a distant future. Professional satisfaction, greater assimilation in the host society, and a settled, comfortable lifestyle added to the reluctance to go back. Having grown away from the old home in India while getting settled in the new location, many of them did not want to go through the dislocation of moving back to India. But the myth of return remained alive. Few ceased to dream of returning home, but greater personal autonomy and the settled way of life with few familial pressures made permanent settlement more attractive.

Acquiring a new citizenship was a drastic step for the migrants that put a symbolic end to the possibility of return. But as their children came of age as young British and American citizens, with no intention of going to a home that existed largely in their parents' memories, the first generation migrants began initiating the naturalisation procedures. For many it was a difficult emotional decision that meant cutting off ties with the homeland. It was an issue that mainly concerned first generation migrants. Those living in former British colonies had already made their decision regarding nationality by the mid 1970s after the Kenyan and Ugandan crisis. Dual citizenship came to be seen as the device that would lessen the sense of loss at giving up Indian citizenship.

Migration became a part of the Punjabi heritage in the last century, and most of the migrants kept up regular contact with their homes in Punjab through the chain migrations. Indians in Britain and Canada talk of eventually returning home, but very few do return, and an even smaller number stay on at home. But they are not willing to cut off the ties with the homeland, the village that gave them their identity. Nor are they ready to forgo their share in the ancestral agricultural property that they would lose on giving up Indian citizenship.

As the British and American Indian communities became prosperous, the more prominent Indians came in contact with visiting Indian politicians. Over time as Indian politicians of all hues began traveling abroad, the overseas Indians became more influential. For many years overseas Indians had accosted every visiting Indian dignitary with the demand for dual citizenship. Overseas Indians complained about the petty harassment when they traveled to India, bureaucratic red tape and the plethora of foreign exchange regulations. They found it intensely discomfiting to be treated as foreigners in India. No Indian leader gave a categorical response to the demand; most declined to commit themselves while being lavishly dined and feted by the local Indian community.

The question of dual citizenship was discussed extensively at the time of Independence when the nature of nationality was being debated. The Indian nationalists had great sympathy for the overseas Indians. The Indian National Congress set up overseas department and sent study groups to the colonies to look into the conditions of the Indians abroad. When the Congress party formulated its policies on overseas Indians, it advised them to 'make Burma, Ceylon, Malaya, Mauritius your home. Your loyalties should be to the country of your adoption.' In the post-Independence period the official view within the government was that as these colonies became independent, they should be persuaded to accept as their citizens the Indians who had spent long years there. The advice given to the Indians abroad was that they should identify with the political aspirations of the local communities and thereby display their commitment to the countries where they were domiciled.

Any idea of dual citizenship was completely ruled out so that there would be no charges of dual loyalties against overseas Indians. The official advice to the Indians in the colonies was to be loyal and belong without reservation to the countries where they were permanent resident. It was realistic advice for the benefit of those living overseas and was meant to safeguard their interests. Speaking in the Constituent Assembly, Jawaharlal Nehru made it clear that if the Indians abroad were not Indian citizens, then India's interest in them was "cultural, humanitarian and not political".

India as a newly independent country had the enormous task of nation building, of creating a sense of nationhood among its disparate peoples. The Indian Constitution incorporated rules of nationality for its citizens that took into account the partition of the country. It made domicile in the territory of India an essential element for citizenship at the commencement of the Constitution. An Indian was one who had his domicile in the territory of India or was born in India, or had been a resident in the territory of India for at least five years before the Constitution was adopted on January 26, 1950.

The Citizenship Act of 1955 defined the terms of citizenship; it provided Indian citizenship to anyone whose father was an Indian citizen, if his or her birth was registered with the Indian High Commission within a year. It extended Indian citizenship to overseas Indians resident in Commonwealth countries (except Pakistan) if they so desired. Most Indians living abroad in the British colonies took the citizenship of the United Kingdom at the time of India's independence. Nationality became a critical issue among migrant communities with the rise of nationalism in the British colonies in Asia and Africa. Independence cut of India from the overseas Indians living in the colonies. The regular traffic between India and the other British colonies was disrupted, especially after the foreign exchange restrictions made it difficult for Indians to travel abroad. It led to a general indifference in India regarding the overseas Indians, aside from the times when they faced discrimination and harassment abroad. India's connections with the overseas communities were mainly through its diplomatic missions in these newly independent nations.

Citizenship issues plagued the Indians in East Africa. In Kenya, the Citizenship Act of 1963 did not confer automatic citizenship even to those eligible for it. Indians had to take an oath relinquishing any previously held citizenship. The Kenyan leaders saw the number of applications for citizenship as a test of loyalty for the entire Indian community, for a substantial number of Indians opted for British citizenship. When the Tanzanian government began tightening its regulations during 1967, the Indian government firmly told the Tanzanians that no person forcibly deported from Tanzania would be allowed into India unless they were Indian citizens. It was to underscore that Indians with British passports were the responsibility of the British government and the matter was between the British and Tanzanian governments. It was meant to protect Indians domiciled abroad.

China, on the other hand, still considered as its nationals all Chinese born anywhere in the world and living in any country. Chinese parentage was Chinese citizenship even if the individual had voluntarily acquired the citizenship of a foreign country. In the later years, this policy created problems for Chinese living in Malaysia and Indonesia, when the dual citizenship facility led to suspicions regarding the loyalties of the Chinese residents. But China's aggressive policy regarding overseas Chinese was not any more effective than India's legalistic stand when it came to the post-independence travails of immigrant communities. China made changes in its policy some years later.

France and Britain allowed dual citizenship, but the United States did not, till a US Supreme Court ruling in 1967 allowed Americans to hold the passport of another country. In America, under the oath taken at the time of naturalisation, the individual pledges to "renounce and abjure absolutely and entirely, all allegiance and fidelity to any foreign prince, potentate, state or sovereignty of which the applicant was before a subject or citizen." The oath stands counter to the concept of dual citizenship, and the US does not have any legislation that provides for dual citizenship. But over the years the United States has developed an administrative policy that, while it does not favour dual citizenship, tolerates its existence. An individual loses his citizenship status only if he formally writes to the authorities to renounce his American citizenship.

With the United States liberalising its regulations, more immigrant communities have begun to seek dual citizenship. Since then countries like Canada, Colombia, Ecuador, Brazil, New Zealand and the Dominican Republic have allowed their citizens to hold two passports. Australia amended its citizenship act in early 2003 to allow dual citizenship for its nationals; earlier, only Australia born nationals could hold two passports. Countries that have a large diasporic community have faced demands for dual citizenship, especially after the US liberalised its regulations. Countries that have a large emigrant population receive substantial remittances from them, and some of them have also made changes in their citizenship regulations.

There had been strong opposition in India to granting dual citizenship. Citizenship was seen as a relationship between a sovereign state and a national, which involved feelings of loyalty and patriotism, and an emotional attachment to a homeland. Holding citizenship of two countries ran counter to the idea of citizenship with the rights and responsibilities that go with that status. The demand for dual citizenship came mainly from first generation Indian migrants. After giving up Indian citizenship and swearing allegiance to another country, the demand for dual citizenship was perceived as duplicitous.

The main reasons for the demand were that it would make travel to India easier by doing away with the need for visas. Secondly it would facilitate the purchase of property in India and finally it was an emotional demand to retain the bond with India. Overseas Indians, particularly those who had become naturalised citizens of the US and UK chaffed at the inconvenience of obtaining Indian visas and paying the differential rates charged from foreign nationals by hotels etc. The opposition was that it went counter to the notions of patriotism, national cohesion and loyalty to one's homeland. It also raised questions regarding the personal law that would be applicable to them. The official view was that dual citizenship would allow overseas militant groups, such as the Khalistani and other insurgent groups the freedom to travel and operate in India without any checks.

The Bharatiya Janata Party (BJP) and its affiliates such as the Vishwa Hindu Parishad and Overseas Friends of BJP had been in close touch with the overseas community for many years. The BJP as the party that stood for a Hindu nation and stressed Indian cultural values attracted the overseas Indians. When the BJP came to power in 1998 as part of the National Democratic Party (NDA) it was faced by a growing demand for dual citizenship from a section of overseas Indians. But Indians at home were not ready for dual citizenship. Unwilling to annoy the overseas Indians in the US and Britain, who were becoming increasingly vociferous in their demand, the government introduced the PIO card.

The PIO card offered many facilities but fell short of dual citizenship. Any person of Indian descent whose parents, grandparents or great grandparents were born in undivided India (before August 15, 1947) was eligible for the PIO card, providing their ancestors had not become citizens of Pakistan or Bangladesh at any time. The PIO card was available to spouses of Indian citizens and those eligible for PIO cards by birth. The card allowed visa free entry into India, and cardholders did not need to register with the Foreigners Registration Officer if they stayed in India for less than 180 days. It allowed the cardholder to acquire and sell land in India for residential or commercial purposes. It allowed the same facilities as were available to Non-Resident Indians, such as admission in educational institutes under the NRI quota. The PIO card was an administrative decision, providing a slew of facilities to the overseas Indians and did not require a Constitutional amendment. But the PIO scheme found few takers because of the high fee and it did not offer any of the privileges that the recipients were looking for. The fee was initially pegged at $ 1000 and later reduced to $ 300.

With the growing involvement of overseas Indians in the politics of the host countries, the overseas community has become immensely influential both at home and abroad. The NDA government had to take the help of prominent Indians in the US and elsewhere to soften the blow of international isolation and economic sanctions that were enforced after India's nuclear tests in 1998. The Indian community helped to put across the Indian point of view to influential opinion and policy makers in the western capitals. It served to increase their influence on the Indian leadership.

In September 2000 the NDA government constituted a High Level Committee for the Indian Diaspora to go into the entire question of the people of Indian origin abroad. The High Level Committee was headed by L.M. Singhvi, a former Indian High Commissioner to the UK, who had been a strong proponent of dual citizenship. The High Level Committee's report presented to the government in 2002 recommended granting of dual citizenship. Prime Minister Atal Bihari Vajpayee agreed to the recommendation but it still took time to overcome bureaucratic resistance to the concept. Initially it was believed that dual citizenship would require an amendment to the Constitution, but Dr. Singhvi, a constitutional expert pointed out that changes in the Indian Citizenship Act would suffice.

At the first *Pravasi Bharatiya Divas* in 2003, Prime Minister Vajpayee told the assembled gathering of overseas Indians that India would introduce dual citizenship for Indians living in about eight countries. The bill was hurriedly passed on the last day of the Winter Session of Parliament and received Presidential assent in the first week of January. The details of the scheme, colour of the passport, etc were still to be worked out, but the Prime Minister announced the scheme, at the second *Pravasi Divas* on January 9.

Residents of Indian origin in 16 countries were eligible for dual citizenship. These 16 countries that allowed dual citizenship, are Australia, Britain, Canada, Cyprus, Greece, France, Finland, Ireland, Italy, Israel, Netherlands, New Zealand, Portugal, Switzerland, Sweden and USA.

The dual citizenship is on offer only to those who are citizens of countries that allow their citizens to hold two passports. India is in the company of over 80 countries that offer some form of dual citizenship to its people. Much of the opposition to dual citizenship in India was circumvented by offering a different class of citizenship – Overseas Citizen of Indian origin that does not confer political rights on the individual. The dual Indian passport is actually an upgraded PIO card with a few additional privileges that are normally granted to long-term residents in many countries. The citizenship document would provide visa-free travel facility to India but overseas Indians will not be eligible for government jobs, or have the right to vote or contest elections. The dual passport is not a right conferred on all persons of Indian origin and would be granted to the applicant at the government's discretion.

However, the offer of dual citizenship has split the overseas community, it left many of the overseas Indians present at the second *Pravasi Divas* puzzled and disgruntled. Those eligible for dual citizenship welcomed the offer, while others were afraid of its repercussions in the host society. Indians from South Africa and Malaysia found the offer alarming. Indians in South Africa are still trying to find their legitimate space in the new emerging South African society and any suggestion of divided loyalties implied by dual citizenship would destabilise the Indian community in South Africa. The saga of the Asian expulsion from Uganda has still not faded from the memories of Indians in Africa. The government has offered dual citizenship to one section of the overseas community at a time when there are stateless Indians living in countries such as Sri Lanka and Myanmar.

The Outlook magazine in its January 2003 issue quoted an unidentified protestor as saying: "In one stroke we have divided the Indian community abroad in A-class countries and those in B-class countries. Those living in Africa and other places are lesser mortals." A South African Indian explained, "Our ethnic origin haunts us at every turn. We were not white earlier, now we have limited opportunities because we are not black. What are we? South Africans or people of Indian origin? Already when racial abuse is hurled at us, they say go back to where you came from. Dual citizenship will give an edge to those taunts." Indians in countries like Fiji and Malaysia have heard similar taunts at times of racial tension.

It added fuel to a growing impression among the diaspora that the government was more interested wooing the "dollar diaspora" to take into consideration the concerns of the overseas Indians from other countries. The aggressive new migrants from the western countries had hogged most of the speaking time during the discussions leaving the others disgruntled. Since dual citizenship was available to those living mainly in developed countries, the offer added to the general dissatisfaction among the rest of the diaspora, even those who were not worried about its repercussions at home.

The offer of dual citizenship generated mixed feelings even among migrants, according to Prashanth Lakhihal writing in *India Tribune* of Jan. 28, 2003. Without the fundamental right to vote, it is only a namesake, said G. Atmacharan Reddy. Community newspapers wrote of a few community leaders who privately said that the American government could question the loyalty of an individual who has two citizenships. There is a conservative view in the United States that opposes dual citizenship after Mexico's 1998 law that extended citizenship to individuals of Mexican extraction and their children. Conservative critics saw the Mexican law as a plan to export segments of the Mexican population to the

United States, especially when Mexico allowed absentee voting. While dual citizenship gives the advantage of easier movement, purchase of property and inheritance, it has some disadvantages with its implication of a potential lack of diplomatic protection. But for the majority the advantages of dual citizenship outweigh its negative aspects.

Chapter 11

Identity and Assimilation

The diaspora has evolved in various ways in the different countries where Indians are domiciled. The length of time since the act of migration, assimilation in the local society, political awareness and participation in the political process has had its impact on the diasporic sense of identity. Recent migrants have a strong sense of identity as Indians, while third or fourth generation descendants of migrants have multiple and overlapping ideas of their ethnic and national identities. But emotional associations linger on among migrant communities, the ties may lie dormant for years till an event or a memory activates them.

Boodhun Teelock was born in Mauritius and went on to become his country's High Commissioner to London. All he knew about his grandfather, Tilak, was that he had come to Mauritius from India as a young man. Teelock's eldest daughter, Vijaylakshmi was working at the Mahatma Gandhi Institute in Port Louis when she came upon a photograph of her great grandfather among the records of the Indian indentured workers. The photograph generated a lot of excitement within the Teelock family and roused a desire to search for the family's roots. Vijaylakshmi scanned the immigration records maintained by the Institute of the indentured workers. The arrival records showed that Tilak had reached Mauritius in 1863 at the age of 25 years, but gave no further information about his origins. However, the date of arrival was a significant clue and the Teelock family tried to trace links through the National Archives and the Registrar General's Department. They finally managed to locate a copy of Tilak's death certificate, which gave his parents name and his place of birth. It was listed as Burraree village in Bihar.

Boodhun Teelock visited India several times, but it was not easy to find village Burraree in Bihar. He eventually hired a private detective to locate the village. In 1999 Teelock received information that the village was in Siwan district. Though not in good health, 77-year-old Boodhun Teelock travelled to Bihar to visit his ancestral village. The homecoming brought both joy and pain. It was an intensely moving visit but the poverty of the village left a deep imprint in his mind. Talking to people in Burraree Teelock discovered that it did not have a public health centre within easy reach, only the seriously ill were taken to the nearest township for medical attention. "My grandfather started life in Mauritius as a farm worker. He faced difficult times but his hard work paid off. He had acquired 25 acres of land by the time he died. Burraree was the village he came from and I wanted to do something for my grandfather's village." Teelock contacted the District Magistrate of Siwan and made a donation of Rs. 10 lakh for providing health facilities in the village.

Jagdish Shukla, Professor of Climate Change at George Mason University in Virginia, attended the first *Pravasi Bharatiya Sammelan* in Delhi. Shukla, a first generation migrant had just visited his village in eastern Uttar Pradesh. Nothing had changed in the village in all these years, he said, it still took longer to get from Delhi to his village that it did to reach Delhi from America.

Shukla had started work on setting up a school in his village, "Why didn't I do this 25 years ago", he wondered, speculating that much of the complaining about India at the gathering of overseas Indians was motivated by guilt at having left India. Whether it is a 137-year-old tie or merely 25 years that separate the migrant from his roots, the emotional ties do not die out completely.

The question of identity is a knotty one for the migrant who has moved to an alien land. The arrival in a new country was a fearful experience for the indentured worker, uprooted as he was from his home and all that was familiar. Thrown into new surroundings, it was a complete dislocation, which broke the bonds and connections, traditions and customs that had formed a part of his life. The workers struggled to preserve their Indian identity through the trauma of indenture and the brutalisation on the plantations. They tried to recreate lost familial connections by forging new relationships with their shipmates, the '*jahazibhais*', and tried to rebuild their lives within the strange rules in the unfamiliar surroundings. Religion and its rituals gave some meaning to their lives in the harsh, new world and helped to preserve their identity.

Plantation workers would gather for prayer meetings in the '*coolie lines*' on Sundays, the congregations provided social interaction for the tired workers. Religion was their only solace and it was the oral Indian tradition that kept religious beliefs and conventions going. The workers followed the *bhakti* tradition and set up *bhajan mandalis* (group of religious song-singers). They performed *Ramlilas* for the story of Ram's exile and the victory of good over evil was a theme close to their hearts. Few of the workers were literate, and only some of them had carried the *Ramayana* and other religious books when they set out from their homes. Those workers who knew verses from the religious texts were in great demand to lead the religious ceremonies.

The early indenture migrations took place from northern India and it was the local customs and festivals of that region that took hold among the workers. *Holi* and *Diwali* are the two main religious festivals in these countries, though *Holi* is more commonly known as '*Paghwa*' from "*Phag*' as it is called in rural Uttar Pradesh. The *tazia* procession during *Moharram* is not just restricted to Shias and has acquired a much wider appeal in the Caribbean. The practice of putting up coloured flags at the end of a *puja* (worship) became a regular feature. The '*jhandi*' or flag can be seen in front of Indian homes throughout the Caribbean countries, a practice that is followed in some rural communities in India.

As they settled down in the new country after completing their indenture term, they struggled to find a place for themselves in the colonial society. Since the Indians formed a sizeable group, the community turned inwards for its cultural and social sustenance. Within their homes they replicated some of the old values and traditions with a few modifications. They stuck to their traditional patterns in dress, food and manners. But the desperate clinging to the Indian identity and its familiar traditions had a negative impact on the colonial society, for Indians acquired the reputation of being insular and hidebound.

In *The Banyan Tree*, Hugh Tinker wrote: "Do Asians create their own difficulties by their own way of life, and by remaining separate from the host society; or do their troubles arise mainly from excess chauvinism or racism in the country of adoption? Do they offend because they are, visibly, both *pariahs* and exploiters in an alien society? Or are they scapegoats, singled out for victimisation because their adopted country (or its government) needs an alibi for poor performance in the national sphere?" According to Tinker, Indians offend because they are visibly prosperous.

Indians are not the only ones to have faced accusations of being racially exclusive. Overseas Chinese and Japanese have also faced jealousies in their countries of domicile and have been accused of being racially exclusive. Indians tended to focus on the discrimination they faced in the colonial society and never saw themselves as exploiters, even if they dominated the retail trade. The majority were farmers, office workers and wage earners with a few professionals but they were better off than large sections of the local urban population. A small elite group of merchants and traders, usually belonging to the Gujarati community, were visibly affluent, which led to the Indian community being labelled as a prosperous community.

During the 1970s as the colonies gained independence there were loud complaints that Indians were parochial exclusivists. The Indians kept to themselves and except on professional basis, had very little interaction with other ethnic groups. Despising the other minorities, they socialised among themselves and did not marry outside their community. They were accused of being arrogant and exploiting the poor Black population. This was the common image of the Indian community in East Africa and the Caribbean. It was an image fostered by the colonial society by exaggerating some of Indian habits. The colonial authorities consistently kept the different racial groups apart as an administrative convenience and encouraged them to despise the other's values and traditions. Christian missionaries described Indians as heathens who worshipped strange gods. Indians, on the other hand, looked down upon the Blacks as '*junglees*' (uncultured) and feckless people, who avoided hard work.

Asians in Africa perpetuated their class distinctions and ethnic exclusiveness in their social and business dealings. The Europeans believed that they were racially superior to the Africans but the Indians were said to be displaying cultural superiority because of their inordinate pride in their ancient culture. There were loud complaints about Indian exclusiveness and cultural arrogance, but the main cause of ill will was the economic dominance of the Indian community. As independence approached, the Europeans generally adjusted their behaviour towards the Africans according to the changing times, but the Asians were slow to perceive the need to change. They failed to participate wholeheartedly in the rising African nationalism, which added to the rancour at the Indian commercial monopoly in the country.

Colonial society compartmentalised the ethnic groups, but post-colonial societies had to find ways to integrate all sections. In Trinidad of the 1970s the Blacks saw Indians clinging to their culture as being in conflict with the concept of national unity. They considered Black culture as the mainstream culture and ignored or derided Indian cultural forms. But modernisation and western influences became too strong for the third and fourth generation of Indian descent. The ancestral saga of indentured migration had grown too dim to recall. By the third generation the memories of indenture had faded. It was a period that their parents did not want to talk about and it became an academic concept briefly touched upon in the history books. The effects of westernisation became dominant with films, music and entertainment.

Links with India loosened after independence and the main information about India came from western newspapers with their emphasis on floods, droughts and poverty. They did not paint an attractive picture of India. After decades of indifference, even a degree of hostility towards India, there has been a revival of interest in Indian culture, classical dance and music in the recent years. Young people of Indian origin in the Caribbean, Fiji and other places are learning Indian cultural forms. Indian films, music and television have evoked a new interest in their Indian heritage. Many Trinidadians sing accent-free film songs in Hindi without being able to string a complete sentence in the language. Indian films and popular music have revived a desire to learn the old language that was dying out in the urban areas.

First generation migrants in the 20th century were voluntary migrants, who had a strong need to preserve their Indianness for the majority of them planned to return home after a few years. It became even more important when their growing children began getting affected by the western society. The new migrant settled down in his new environment and the newfound prosperity gave him a sense of material well being, but questions of identity kept him unsettled. Some societies frown on alien cultural practices and seek a submerging of all separate identities into a common, dominant, stable society. Most pluralistic societies require a large degree of integration of the ethnic groups, but allow minority groups to retain some parts of their separate identity while developing a common consciousness. In earlier decades the integration would be a form of assimilation where the migrant has to conform to the majority community life. The modern trend is towards accommodation, that is an amalgam of different people tied by some common strands, which allow them to carry on with those of their cultural and religious practices that do not offend the majority.

In Canada and Britain the chain migrations kept alive a social and cultural milieu that was similar to the one at home in India. The social isolation that the early migrants faced in the West ensured that the Asian migrants stuck to each other for support and social interaction. The post-World War II migrations brought changes in the western countries. When the migrants were a small minority, they could be ignored in the expectation that most of them would return home after their work was over. Even as the migrant communities grew larger and more varied, they could be kept out of mainstream society as they mainly lived is their own self-created world. In Britain they were a marginalized community, which was belittled for its overcrowded homes and the strange cooking smells that emanated from its homes.

Indian migrants in Britain, even those in well-paying middle class jobs, found social acceptance difficult within white British society. Aware of the subtle discrimination, South Asians tended to stick to their own ethnic circles. South Asians form almost half of Britain's four million strong immigrant communities. The social exclusion meant that the immigrant Asian community formed their own settlements where they replicated their traditional lifestyles. It is truly said that a South Asian can live his whole life in the UK without needing to learn the English language. After the race riots in 2002, an official report found that in the several towns like Bradford and Oldham there are well-defined Asian areas that are virtually "no-go" areas for non-Asians.

In the last two decades, there has been a growing acknowledgement of the multicultural nature of their societies in countries with large immigrant populations such as Britain, Canada, the US and some European countries. According to the UNDP's Human Development Report for 2004, the number of international migrants (defined as people living outside their country of birth) more than doubled since mid-1970s to about 175 million. The new wave of migration has brought some changes in the concept of cultural diversity and its impact on host societies. At one time, migrants to America were expected to shed their old identities to become Americans in the assimilation or "melting pot" ethos, there has since been a shift to the salad bowl approach of multiculturalism in America that recognises the value of diversity and supports multiple identities.

The changing ethos has allowed Indians to preserve their cultural identity and religion. Hinduism prescribes the rituals and practices of ordinary day-to-day life in the dress, food habits and the ritual purity associated with food, language and behavioural patterns. Muslims follow traditional patterns of life that they are loath to give up, particularly for the decadent lifestyles of modern, western societies. It is the children of migrants who have to find ways to deal with the conflicting customs they find outside their homes and the traditional values and behaviour expected of them at home. Some second-generation migrants manage to reconcile the two arenas they operate in, the home and the outside world, modifying their behaviour to fit either arena. For others, the search for an identity in the country of birth adds a sharper dimension to the problems of growing up in a Western society.

Distinctive ethnic traits can often be seen even in the third or fourth generation, though they may be traces that become apparent only on special days, in the special foods or ethnic dress for festive occasions. But language usually begins to fade away by the third generation. Second generation migrants are usually bilingual, but their children retain just a smattering of the old language, unless they live in a predominantly Indian locality.

There are two major stages in assimilation and most Indian migrants have traversed the first stage fairly successfully. Cultural assimilation involves accepting the value system and behavioural modes of the adopted society. Indians have accepted the core values of the American system but the majority are still to adopt the second stage that involves a greater participation in mainstream cultural activities. Many western societies have a tradition of volunteer work, which involves them in the local civic affairs. Indians with growing children are very involved in their children's education at home but rarely participate in social and extra-curricular activities in which other parents are involved.

Natasha Pappu wrote in a New York based weekly, *News India Times* of April 11, 2003 "Why is it that I have never seen an Indian name on the contributors list for the St Louis Museum of Art, the Science Museum, the Missouri Botanical Garden or the St Louis Zoo? Why is it that Indians do not run for local office? Why do we seldom volunteer to serve on our children's school boards? —— Until we take the initiative and cross the line from being beneficiaries to active participants – do not begin to contribute to the community in which we live, the community will not welcome us wholeheartedly." Indians are getting involved in politics by contributing time and money to election campaigns. But Natasha

Pappu's complaint questions the community's reluctance to become part of activities that they do not consider essential or prestigious.

In the past decade or more, the more significant cultural evolution among the overseas Indians is the move towards religiosity, especially in the United States, Britain and Canada. Religion has always been central to keeping alive the cultural identity and has been the means of transmission of cultural traits to the second and third generation. The move towards religiosity is often meant to counter the effect of the westernisation on the children of Indian migrants. It has created fertile grounds for religious appeals by orthodox, even reactionary groups. Religious leaders and preachers are regular visitors on the international circuit and religious paraphernalia like *murtis* (statues), books, religious calendars and diaries; materials for religious rituals are fairly easily available. Temples were initially a place for religious and social contact but have grown into an elaborate public expression of Hinduism.

The Vishwa Hindu Parishad set up its American branch in the 1970s catering to the religious needs of the Indians in the US. They fulfilled a need among the Indian migrants whose children, growing up in America were beginning to ask questions about their Indian heritage. The RSS built contacts with the overseas community providing religious connectivity with India. Instead of the new influences helping in reform of religious tradition, the immigrant communities have sometimes regressed to the more conservative beliefs. In 1995 when the message of the *Ganesh miracle* flashed through Indian communities abroad, Hindus rushed to local temples to affirm the marvel that *Ganesh* idols were drinking milk proffered by the devout. The *Ganesh* 'miracle' story reached New York, Hong Kong and other cities through phone calls and fax messages at almost the same time as the news was travelling through India. It showed the spread and speed of connectivity with India and the unquestioning acceptance of obscurantist beliefs.

Indians have, however adapted to the American parade style

of celebration and pageantry marks most Indian cultural celebrations. Dances, songs, speeches, fashion shows are a major part of the celebrations, whether it is India Day or *Diwali*. Such occasions allow a large number of Indians to participate in the activities and also provide some Indians the means to assume a leadership role in community organisations. The Indian migrant has arrived when he has brought an expensive car and a huge house adorned with big photographs of himself in the company of local bigwigs and begins to entertain visiting Indian politicians, artists and other celebrities.

Ethnic Indian social and religious events tend to become the venue for self-promotion. A common characteristic of immigrants is the need to seek recognition of their achievements; it is what makes the dislocation from the homeland a worthwhile enterprise. The American lifestyle lays considerable emphasis on individual achievements. Indians who take the decision to migrate are also individualistic and adapt well to this aspect of American life. For many migrant Indians the recognition of their personal success is even more important than the success itself.

Promoting oneself is seen as acceptable behaviour in the American milieu and translates into a self-congratulatory style among Indians. Self-promotion has led to multiplicity of Indian organisations in the United States and is the reason for the multitude of Indians who clamour for appreciation and acknowledgement at Indian community functions. Office bearers of different Indian associations made a sorry spectacle by fighting among themselves to reach the microphone at a function in New York organised for the then Prime Minister Atal Bihari Vajpayee.

Factions break out from Indian organisations in the same way as political parties fragment in India. Individuals feeling left out of leadership roles take their friends and associates out of the parent group to start their own set-up. There are now two parades in New York on August 15 to celebrate India's independence day and even a lawsuit on the routes to be taken by the two parades. Organisations continue to split over minor or personal issues, on regional and class lines as individuals build up resentment against domination by other groups.

The Indian community in the United States, Britain, Canada, Netherlands, Australia and New Zealand is not a cohesive or homogenous community, for it reflects the diversity of Indian life. New migrants exhibit different traits and attitudes from older migrants or second-generation migrants. Another separate group, which finds few areas of common interest with emigrants from India, are the second time migrants.

The second time migrants are a distinct group of secondary migrants who have reached the United States, Britain, Canada, Netherlands and Australia through Mauritius, East Africa, Fiji or the Caribbean. There is also a difference between direct migrants to UK and those who had arrived from East Africa. Most Indians who went from East Africa had some trading or commercial skills as well as some amount of capital when they arrived in Britain. They quickly moved into small enterprises like the cornershops and newsagents shops. The Gujarati family networks helped to raise the initial capital required to start new enterprises and it is this class of migrants who have contributed the largest number of millionaires among the Indian community in the United Kingdom. The direct migrants were workers or professionals, and while they have also done well for themselves, they do not match the entrepreneurship skills or affluence of the East African Asians.

The second time migrants frequently feel alienated from the direct migrants, who they find, not only arrogant but ignorant as well. Indians in the Caribbean and in Fiji have maintained their ancestral language against great odds. But language evolves and changes with time and a variety of influences. The Hindustani spoken by these overseas Indians is drawn from the language their forefathers took from India. It carries a miscellany of words and phrases from the dialects of rural India of the late 19th and early 20th century. It can sound strange and old fashioned to young Indians, whose own spoken language is heavily influenced by Indian films. These third and fourth generation Indians are often made to feel awkward and embarrassed about their ungrammatical Hindustani by the prattle of the direct migrants.

Many Indians have no knowledge of the patterns of Indian migration and the existing Indian settlements around the world. The Indo-Caribbean cultural identity, like the Indo-Fijian identity to a lesser extent, has been influenced by the prevailing customs in those countries. They are also influenced by popular western and African culture. Migrants from India find these traits odd and unIndian. They make no effort to hide the fact that they do not consider them true Indians and do not wish to associate with the Indo-Guyanese or the Indo-Trinidadians. "These Indians are ignorant, they have no idea about the Indian communities in the Caribbean and they act like they look down on us. Most of us try to keep away from these Indians from India," said Jay Gobind, a young immigrant from Trinidad.

A Fiji-Indian living in Sydney complained that Indians newly arrived from India had an air of superiority – almost like a person from a developed country coming in contact with a poor migrant from a Third World country. At any function organised for people of Indian origin, it is the Indian migrants who take over the function and focus mainly on issues of interest to them. They have no interest in the conditions of Indians in Fiji, even though the Fiji-Indians form a major part of the Indian community in Sydney. Auckland has the largest concentration of Indians from Fiji, but "these new arrivals from India treat us like uncouth *junglees* (uncultured)."

There is clearly a need to build a common overseas Indian identity, bringing together the different strands of the multiple Indian migrations around the world. The Indian diaspora will gain in importance if it incorporates all sections of people of Indian descent in a well-networked international presence around the globe.

Chapter 12

Politics and the Diaspora

The Indian diaspora, settled in large numbers in several countries for over a century, have faced a long battle against political marginalisation. By the 1990s people of Indian origin had acquired high political positions in the countries where they had settled. The diaspora had three Presidents of Indian origin, three Prime Ministers, 68 Ministers and over 250 Members of Parliament around the globe as well as half a dozen British Peers of Indian descent. Canada had six Indian Canadians in its Parliament and Ujjal Dossanjh was elected Premier of British Columbia Province in that period. Three Indians were elected to the State Legislatures in the US elections in 2003. Two of them were re-elected for a second term and the third; Swati Dandkar warded off an opposition challenge, which questioned her ability to represent American mid-western values as an immigrant.

With enterprise and political skills Indians have headed governments in countries where they form a substantial part of the population such as Fiji, Trinidad and Tobago, Suriname and Guyana. But they have lost power in these five countries, either through violent means or through presidential action. In Mauritius where Indians are 70 per cent of the country's population, political power was transferred to a Prime Minister of Franco-Mauritian descent, Paul Berenger, of the Mauritius Militant Movement (MMM) in 2003 through a political power-sharing arrangement with his predecessor. In mid 2000 an armed gang in Fiji captured Mahendra Chaudhry, the country's first Prime Minister of Indian descent, with the intention of restoring political power to the indigenous Fijians. A year later across the globe in the Caribbean, Trinidad and Tobago's first Prime Minister of Indian descent Basdeo Pandey lost office when the President chose to appoint his opponent to the job after a tied election result. Several decades earlier, the Cheddi Jagan government was dismissed in Guyana in 1953 while the country was on the path to self-rule with the result that the Indo-Guyanese remained in political isolation for almost four decades. In Suriname, the military strongman, Col Desi Bouterse's second coup in 1990 threw out President Ramsewak Shankar's government.

Are these instances an indication of a distinct antagonism to Indian politicians? Why are Indian led governments unstable and easily deposed? According to Dr. L. M. Singhvi, Chairman of the High Level Committee on the Diaspora explained, "The circumstances in each country are different, each problem is different and the problems are complex. They are a legacy of history and the complexity of the problem increases because of the diversity in the small countries. They cannot be generalised."

These instances, however, have a degree of similarity, which can provide the reasons why all the Indian led governments have lost power in ethnically bipolar states. Ethnicity forms a strong element in the politics of these countries, where there is no single dominant ethnic group. But it would be a simplistic notion to blame the ousters solely on racial motives, for each occasion has its distinct circumstances, even though the Indian origin of the leader forms a significant contributing factor. Each of these countries has different ethnic segments, which changes the complexion of the ethnic rivalry. As long as parties remain dominated by one ethnic group, competition for power will have strong racial overtones.

In these former plantation economies, Indians were treated as the perpetual outsiders during the colonial period, later they came to be seen as competitors for political power because of the size of the Indian population. One reason for the vulnerability of Indian led governments that does not depend on race is that they are usually the outsiders – newcomers to governance and have to deal with an existing establishment that is intensely suspicious of change. The new leaders do not have the backing of the instruments of state: the administration, the bureaucracy, the security forces or even the big business interests. Hence, they are easily destabilised by those opposed to their government. The limited Indian presence in the armed forces makes it easier to use them to oust Indian led governments. The coups in the Caribbean and the South Pacific were facilitated by the fact that there are few Indians in the security services of these countries.

In the Caribbean the Africans have dominated the armed forces. During the colonial times, certain professions became the spheres of different communities. Most of these countries have invisible barriers towards the Indians joining the armed forces. In Fiji, the army was almost entirely ethnic Fijian. When the bar against Indians was removed, the physical requirements of height and chest measurements for a new recruit were stipulated in a manner that effectively rendered the smaller built Indians ineligible for selection. At the same time, there is also the fact that young Indians did not see the security forces as an attractive career option, so they did not make concerted efforts to break the barrier to their entry into the forces. Indians have, however managed to enter the police force in small numbers.

Indian Prime Ministers carry with them the baggage of being

"Indian origin". In the multi-racial societies where Indians form a sizeable part of the population, an Indian can be elected leader only with the support of a significant section of non-Indians. But his opponents have used his ethnic identity to paint him as a leader of the Indian community, who has displaced the long standing ruling party through ethnic support, rather than his party's policies and political appeal. The prosperity of a small Indian elite is portrayed as the norm for the Indian community and used to arouse envy and ire among other sections of society. The latent antipathy towards the Indian community is hammered into visible hostility by harping on Indians being rich businessmen exploiting the poor people in the country. The Indian community is not always homogenous, and the fragmented leadership among the Indians makes it easy for opponents to divide them. In Trinidad, Basdeo Panday lost his majority in a leadership struggle within his government.

In these small nation states, the political stakes are high in terms of the fruits of office. When Indians are politically marginalised, they are also kept out of top jobs in the bureaucracy and other fields of employment as well as government patronage such as contracts and business opportunities. Individuals may still strike personal alliances with the ruling establishment, but the Indian community tends to lose its influence over policy making. Though race relations are not hostile in these multiracial societies, election time accentuates the ethnic differences, which get exploited when there is a change in government. Indian led governments will be short-lived as long as they depend on a single ethnic base. In the multi-ethnic societies political stability can be ensured only through wider political alliances.

Colonial administrations ruled through keeping the ethnic groups at a distance from each other and these entrenched patterns of social interaction are still to fade away. In the colonies the initial political activity among the Indians flowed from the fight for the rights of the sugarcane farmers and the battle to get recognition for Hindu marriages. The early political activity was on ethnic, community issues; later politics in these countries followed ethnic lines with each ethnic group forming its own political party. After independence, political parties made efforts to widen their support base, but the main parties are still dominated by one or the other community.

In British Guiana, Cheddi Jagan's government was dismissed by the colonial administration because of his communist beliefs. Cheddi Jagan's coalition of working class Indians and Africans won a surprise victory in the elections, but the PPP government's policies upset powerful sections, including the Brooks Corporation that owned the major plantations in the country. A three-week long strike on the sugar estates led the government to introduce a Labour Relations bill in the legislature. Cheddi Jagan's socialist philosophy and admiration of Moscow's policies had sent alarm bells ringing in Britain and America.

It was the height of the Cold War, at a time when North Korea had marched into South Korea, and the United States did not want another Cuba like situation in its backyard. The Iranian government of Prime Minister Mohammed Mossadegh had been toppled in the same year in a CIA backed operation because of his nationalistic, left leaning views. The local papers in Georgetown were running a campaign against the Labour Relations bill calling it a creeping communist takeover. Finally, the British government dismissed the PPP government, landed British troops in Georgetown and assumed emergency powers.

The People's Progressive Party was the broadbased combination of political groups that were leading the demand for self-rule. Linden Forbes Burnham was the leader of the urban African workers in the PPP but the colonial powers incited an ambitious Forbes Burnham to form a separate group, the People's National Congress. They made much of a so-called perceived assertiveness among the Indians ever since India became independent in 1947. Africans were led to believe that the Indian leaders hoped to become closer to India and take Guyana into India's sphere of influence. Jagan became Premier after the 1961 elections but the country remained destabilised through long drawn out strikes and industrial action, making it difficult to run the government.

In the 1964 elections, though the PPP got 46 per cent of the votes, Burnham with 40 per cent votes aligned with big business backed United Front party to become the Premier. The racial divide became an integral factor in Guyanese politics, with voting taking place mainly on racial lines. Burnham controlled the government till his death in 1985 because of his hold on the largely African army and bureaucracy. After Burnham's death, the new government did away with the fraudulent overseas voting that had helped keep Burnham in power. The elections in 1992 were relatively fair and Cheddi Jagan was elected President. Jagan remained in office till his death in 1997 when his American born wife, Janet Jagan, who had been one of the prime forces in the setting up of the PPP, took over. Bharrat Jagdeo was elected as President in the next elections in 1999 with a substantial majority.

Neighbouring Suriname's spells of civilian rule have been relatively short, interspersed as they were by two coups at a decade's interval. Suriname has a wider ethnic mix in its population, from descendants of African slaves, and indentured workers from Java, India and China. Its politics has been different from the other countries where politics and political parties have polarised between two large ethnic groups. The wider ethnic mix in the population meant that single race based parties had to align with larger combinations of political parties. But "*apan jaat*" (own community) politics dominated in Suriname, the three major ethnic groups, Africans, Indian and Javanese had their own political groups, some purely community based and some progressive formations dominated by one or other ethnic group.

The Indians were never united under one political party, but were spread over several splinter groups and hence did not yield the kind of influence on Suriname's politics that their numbers (37 per cent of the population) would have allowed. The Indian community had opposed the independence of Suriname for fear of ascendancy of the Black community. The combination of a Black dominated army and political leaders making racist remarks were unnerved the Indian community.

A coup led by Sergeant Desi Bouterse on 25 February 1980 ended a succession of weak coalition governments. The army rule was initially welcomed for the stability it brought, but its erratic policies during that period impoverished the ordinary people. The military junta nominated a civilian Prime Minister to govern, but the government lacked coherent political direction and the army kept a considerable presence in the decision making bodies. It flirted with socialist nationalism, choosing Cuba and Grenada as allies, but the US invasion of Grenada in 1983 ended the regime's adventurism. Despite being resource rich, Suriname's economy suffered during this period especially as the Dutch government stopped all assistance.

A new constitution was adopted after a referendum in 1987. The three main political parties representing the Indians, Africans and those of Javanese descent came together under the banner of the Front for Democracy and Development to contest the elections that year. The Front won 40 of the 51 seat National Assembly while the military backed National Democratic Party won only two seats. Ramsewak Shankar who had been Agriculture Minister at the time of the military takeover was elected President. Though the civilian government took over, the military had remained a strong force in decision-making. On December 24,1990 Col Bouterse's army captured the TV station, staging another coup to dislodge Ramsewak Shankar's government.

In Fiji two governments with a large Indian presence were violently overthrown within a period of 13 years. The two violent events followed a curiously similar pattern; armed men stormed into Parliament House and captured the Prime Minister and his Cabinet, both times with the same slogan: Fiji for the (ethnic) Fijians. In 1987, Col Sitiveni Rabuka overthrew Timoci Bavadra's government in an army coup, but the May 2000 armed action was carried out by a few disgruntled individuals and was not backed by the armed forces. Led by George Speight, a failed businessman, the armed gang planned to bring in a more malleable regime and went on to make common cause with hardline indigenous Fijian groups. The army in Fiji is almost entirely ethnic Fijian and while it did not back the armed action, it did not take direct action to restore Mahendra Chaudhry's government.

For 17 years after its independence in 1970, Fiji was lauded for its multi-racial harmony. It had a multi-racial government headed by Ratu Sir Kamisese Mara, a high chief of the indigenous Fijians. In 1987 the Alliance Party lost the elections to the newly formed Labour Party, which was formed to oppose the economic policies of the Alliance government. It was a combination of urban trade unions, with both Indian and ethnic Fijian members, and a section of the Indian sugarcane farmers. Dr. Timoci Bavadra, an ethnic Fijian became Prime Minister but his government was overthrown a month later in a coup that aimed to restore power to the Fijians. The Governor General, Ratu Sir Penaia Ganilau appointed a council of advisors, which included Ratu Mara to run the administration. Though Sitiveni Rabuka was kept out of direct involvement in the government, the army retained a major say in government functioning. After the coup, Indians migrated in large numbers to Australia, New Zealand, Canada and the United States, leading to a drastic economic downturn in Fiji.

A new constitution was adopted in 1990 that reduced the number of Indian seats in Parliament and reserved top posts in government for the ethnic Fijians. After the elections Rabuka split the main ethnic Fijian party and took the support of the Labour

Party, by then headed by Mahendra Chaudhry to form the government. Even though Indians were numerically marginalized in Parliament, it became clear that the country could not progress without the involvement of both the major ethnic groups.

A constitutional review commission prepared a new, racially equitable constitution with a racially fixed membership in the House of Representatives that was pegged to the ethnic proportion in the population. The House of Representatives has 71 members, of which 46 are reserved seats to be elected on communal basis: 23 by ethnic Fijians, 19 by Indians and 3 by General Electors and 1 by the Council of the island of Rotuma. The rest (25 seats) are open seats contested on a common roll. But Rabuka lost the 1999 elections to a winning coalition and package of economic reforms put together by Mahendra Chaudhry.

Chaudhry's government lasted just one year in office. While he was held captive, the crisis was labelled an Indian versus Fijian problem, but once the hostages were released, the factionalism among the Fijian tribes came out in the open. The army mutinied and ethnic Fijians took over airports, hotel resorts, police stations demanding a better return for their land. The army appointed an Interim Government under Laisenia Qarase, a former banker. Several months later a Fiji High Court judge ruled that the dismissal of the Chaudhry Government was illegal and fresh elections were held in September 2001.

During the election, Fiji's electorate was sharply polarized and the moderates in both communities were defeated. Qarase formed the government with the help of the Conservative Alliance, the radical Fijian group that had fielded Speight in the elections. Speight won his election while in prison but was unseated, as he could not take the oath in Parliament.

Once known as the Land of the Hummingbird, Trinidad is the most cosmopolitan of West Indian societies. It has an integrated multiracial society, but election time brings out the ethnic differences since race plays an important role in Trinidad politics. The two main political parties in Trinidad were originally formed along racial lines in the pre-independence period and still continue to appeal mainly to their own ethnic communities. The People's Democratic Party grew out of the joint action by Hindu groups to obtain legal recognition for Hindu religious marriages. It used religion as a binding feature among the Hindus and brought in the sugar workers unions in its ambit. Politics was set along communal lines and the People's National Movement (PNM) led by Dr. Eric Williams was the African party.

In the early decades after independence from Britain in 1962, the PNM dominated the political scene. According to the Indo-Trinidadians, Dr. William's government had a policy to marginalise the Indian community. Though he retained a couple of Indians in his Cabinet, the main part of the community was kept out of political power. The largest employer, the bureaucracy was not open to young Indians. Funds allocation to projects geared for the ethnic Indian community, including schools for Indians, was meagre.

The international oil boom of the mid 1970s gave the Trinidad government a substantial jump in its revenues. International sugar prices were also ruling high and the sudden injection of money in the country had an impact in slowly widening circles. However, the Indians believed that the PNM government was using the extra funds for schemes and projects for the Africans. The period of high revenue did not last too long, by the mid 1980s an economic recession had set in and the PNM was defeated by a multi-racial alliance in the1986 elections.

At the time of independence the Indian community was still a backward one, but by the 1980s it had begun getting active in politics. It was the charismatic, trade union leader, Basdeo Panday who infused a new sense of activism among the Indians and aligned with smaller groups for greater influence. The Indian party made an entry into the government when the People's National

Movement lost the 1986 election to a coalition led by ANR Robinson of the National Alliance for Reconstruction. Prime Minister Robinson and his Finance Minister Basdeo Panday carried out tough IMF backed economic reforms to stem the economic decline through its five-year term. It was during this period that the Black Muslims carried out their revolt by taking Prime Minister Robinson hostage and capturing the radio station.

The economic reforms that cut down government spending, hit the common people hard, with the result that the alliance lost to the PNM in the 1991 election. A People's National Movement government under Patrick Manning remained in power till the next elections. In 1995 Manning made way for Basdeo Panday to become Prime Minister. During Dr. Williams' era it was considered unthinkable that there could ever be a Prime Minister of Indian origin in Trinidad. By the 1990s the situation had undergone a major change. A former trade union leader, Panday had made judicious alliances and mounted a strong challenge during the election campaign with a populist programme that appealed to a wider cross section of voters. Robinson joined the government as minister extraordinare till he was elected President in 1997.

Five years later, Pandey was elected for a second time with a narrow majority. The second Panday government lasted less than a year. It fell due to internal party politics when three Cabinet Ministers resigned, making charges of corruption against the government. The Attorney General, Ramesh Lawrence Maharaj gave a statement that he had lost confidence in the government's ability and commitment to deal effectively with the issue of corruption. Elections were announced in December 2001 after Basdeo Panday lost his majority. The group of three Ministers who had resigned formed a new party called Team Unity, but failed to win their seats in the elections.

The election resulted in an 18:18 tie in the 36-member House of Representatives. As the incumbent Prime Minister Panday expected to stay on and proposed a power sharing arrangement but agreed with Manning to let the President decide on whom to call to form the government. President Robinson chose to invite Patrick Manning to head the government, without giving any reason for his decision. It was a decision that the UNC found difficult to accept and led to a lot of heartburn among the Indian community, for it revived the memories of discrimination during the long PNM rule.

The political deadlock continued for ten months. The sharp polarisation resulted in an unworkable Parliament for the House of Representatives could not elect a Speaker despite several efforts. It meant that government could not obtain Parliamentary approval for its budget and government functioning was paralysed. Parliament met for the third time in August. Silence prevailed when the Clerk of the House called the House to elect a Speaker to be elected. Finally Prime Minister Manning rose to announce that he would ask for the dissolution of the House and fresh elections. With the fiscal year ending in Trinidad on September 30, a new budget had to be approved by Parliament before the end of October.

The third elections in as many years were held on September 7, 2002. The PNM won 20 seats against the 16 that went to the UNC and Patrick Manning became an elected Prime Minister as against the "appointed" Prime Minister he had been for ten months. It was a highly charged political battle between the two parties and their leaders, becoming increasingly acrimonious in the last two years. Fortunately, the elections took place without the intimidation and violence that had been predicted by some observers during the election campaign. The face-off had taken its toll on the UNC, which was seen as the cause of the political instability. Basdeo's confrontational style within the government lost him support among his political colleagues. Three acrimonious elections in three years marred the picture of a politician and community leader who has been a staunch advocate of national unity, opposing any form of racial animosity.

Political assertion by the Indian community and the search for wider cross-ethnic support ended the People's National Movement's long domination of Trinidad's politics. But in both Fiji and Trinidad, leaders of Indian origin lost elections in September 2001 and October 2002 when politics in these two island nations got polarised between the two main ethnic groups. Chaudhry had built up the Labour Party and put together a winning combination in 1999, but a combative style that is effective in the opposition becomes a liability while running a multi-racial government. For stable governments overseas Indian politicians require a support base that cuts across racial lines to the extent that the more radical, ethnic forces are rendered largely powerless. The politics of inclusion require greater tact to avoid alienating different sections of opinion. As Basdeo Panday said after his defeat: "We all have to travel in the same taxi."

Seewoosagar Ramgoolam was the towering leader in Mauritius, who remained Prime Minister for 20 years. In 1982 the Labour Party lost to the leftist Movement Militant Mauricien (MMM) and Anerood Jugnauth became Prime Minister, but a year later Jugnauth formed the Militant Socialist Movement (MSM). Political power in Mauritius has oscillated between Anerood Jugnauth's MSM party and the Labour Party led by Navinchandra Ramgoolam. The last election was a close one. In 2000 Aneroodh Jugnauth arrived at a pre-election arrangement with Paul Berenger's Mauritian Militant Movement to divide the Prime Minister's term between them. The coalition won a resounding victory gaining 57 of the 60 seats in Parliament. Anerood Jugnauth became the Prime Minister with Berenger as Deputy Prime Minister and Finance Minister. Berenger's party had been a junior party in a series of coalitions with various political parties.

After three years as Prime Minister Jugnauth stepped down in favour of Berenger according to the terms of their agreement. In

September 2003 Paul Berenger became the first non-Indian Prime Minister of Mauritius. A month later, the 73-year old veteran politician, Aneroodh Jugnauth was elected to the largely ceremonial position of President in the October 7 presidential election. Earlier in the year, Jugnauth had resigned as head of the MSM party and appointed his son, Pravind Jugnauth as leader of the party. The appointment paved the way for Pravind Jugnauth to be given the post of Deputy Prime Minister as part of the arrangement with Berenger.

There was some grumbling among conservative Hindu leaders that the leadership was going outside the community in an Indian dominated country, but the changeover took place smoothly in September. Minority groups like the Muslims, the African-Creoles and the Chinese supported the change that represented a new era in Mauritius politics. The majority in a harmonious multi-ethnic society have to learn to accommodate the aspirations of the minority groups. It is the nature of Parliamentary politics that minority groups are able to leverage their smaller numbers into highly influential positions in Parliament. In Trinidad and Fiji, Indian leaders have aligned with other political parties to form the government even though they belonged to the minority community.

In the early years of migration to countries like Canada, Britain and the US, the Indian migrants kept out of mainstream politics. The early migrants were not interested in local politics; they had to put all their energies in making a living in the new land. Their immediate concerns were issues that pertained directly to the welfare of the Indian community such as immigration issues and discriminatory practices. The Sikh community conducted long campaigns for recognition of their right to wear beards and turbans. Their political arena was the community organisation, temple and gurdwara politics. The Indian communities were by and large slow to involve in politics. In the United States it was rich Indians, usually doctors, who became politically active through making contributions to election campaigns of individual politicians.

Young educated Indian migrants came from the sections of Indian society that did not concern themselves with civic issues. The emphasis on education in their young lives generally made them apolitical; they seldom had any exposure to the political process in India where the middle classes rarely take the trouble to vote in the elections. For this class of society, taking part in political activity is restricted to professional or trade organisations while participation in social activities is for those who have retired. The Federation of Indians in America and the National Federation of Indians in America were Indian organisations representing Indian immigrants of the professional class. They served social and cultural needs and lobbied on issues pertaining to the Indians. As the community grew, a plethora of organisations sprouted up, on religious and parochial basis, and later on caste, language and community basis. Political awakening among the Indians began in the late 1980s.

It was the IT boom that identified Indians as an affluent community in the US with a high disposable income. According to Chidanand Rajghatta in *The Horse that Flew*, the Clinton White House reached out to the Silicon Valley techies. At one Indian fundraiser Bill Clinton urged the Indian community to broaden and deepen its involvement in American politics. It is the second-generation Indian migrants who have begun to be involved in politics in the civic bodies and at the state and federal level. Indian activism in America led to the formation of the India Caucus in the US Congress. It is due to the recognition achieved by the Indian community that American law-makers have joined the India Caucus in large numbers so as to make it the largest such body in the US Congress.

In Canada and Britain, Indians have begun to participate in the country's politics and Indian communities are wooed by the political parties as influential minority groups. In Canada the concentration of Indian settlers in some constituencies have given the community an added significance for the mainstream political parties that it would not have had if it were spread through the entire country. It has helped to get Indian concerns attended to and resulted in Indian getting elected to the legislatures. An active involvement in local politics by an immigrant community is an important step in its acceptance and assimilation in the host country.

Chapter 13

The Diaspora's Influence

The overseas Indian community has had an unacknowledged but significant influence on Indian society almost since regular emigration began in the 19th century. Over the years, the diaspora's impact has spread through wide areas of economic activity and has also influenced cultural and social mores as also as political thought in the country. Mahatma Gandhi honed his strategy of satyagraha in South Africa and used it during India's freedom struggle. Gandhi, Nehru and Rabindranath Tagore visited Burma, Ceylon and Malaya to involve Indians in the struggle against British imperialism. During the Sino-Indian war of 1962, the Indian government welcomed contributions from the Indians living in East Africa for the war effort.

The relatively low level of contact between the diaspora and the homeland of the earlier years has now grown into a regular and at times even intense interaction. The size and affluence of the diaspora has increased its influence at home, capturing the imagination of a large section of urban and semi-urban youth with its well-acclaimed successes. But diasporic influence can be a mixed blessing, as it can be beneficial as well as detrimental for the mother country.

Remittances have a far-reaching impact on the character and structure of the recipient society and its economy. It is even more evident in places where chain migration has spread the remittance economy over a large area. The short term and seasonal workers from Tamil Nadu and Andhra brought back their earnings to their village homes. On the Coromondal coast of the Bay of Bengal, Calingapatnam was once a busy, bustling port with regular shipping to Rangoon. Buddhist relics excavated in the vicinity give credence to the local belief that Buddhism travelled from Calingapatnam to Sri Lanka and Japan. But Calingapatnam has now settled down to being a sleepy, fishing village in the decades after the Rangoon traffic came to an end.

The older women in the Coromondal coast still sing songs of those days: "My beloved has gone to Rangoon, he will come back with silver trinkets for my daughters. May Goddess Poleramma look after him and bring him back to me." In those days Rangoon was the glittering, bright city of lights that beckoned the youth from the Coromondal shores and scores of young men paid Rs 14 for a passage to Rangoon. According to the fraying harbour records, 181 ships put into port in the year 1937-38, that is more than three ships a week carrying goods and passengers across the seas. The prosperity of the region, which came from the remittances and trade with Burma, dwindled after the diasporic traffic dried up.

The diaspora has had a deep-rooted impact in Punjab through more than a hundred years of migration from the villages of Punjab to foreign lands right across the globe. In her book, The Making of Little Punjab in Canada, Archana B Verma quoted a Punjab Banking Committee report for 1929-30 that gave the daily average inward remittance through the Jalandhar branch of the Imperial Bank as Rs 5000. Several districts saw chain migration of villagers going to join relatives working abroad. Most of the migrants kept in touch with their families in India and there was a good deal of to-and-fro traffic on that route. The impact of foreign remittances has changed village life. People with relatives' abroad vie for new ranking in status and seek to increase their influence and power in the community. Conspicuous consumption has become a pattern in the rural districts with high levels of emigration. Land values have risen to levels that take it out of the reach of local residents who have no access to remittance income.

Villages in Hoshiarpur district have sprawling bungalows dotted with air conditioners and a couple of sleek cars parked in front, but very few young people to enjoy the luxuries. Almost every family in these villages has one or more members living abroad. Jagvinder Kaur has her cousin's children living with her for company. "My elder son was desperate to go abroad so I sold two acres of farmland to pay the travel agent. Four years later he sent for his younger brother and I had to pawn my jewellery to buy the ticket. But they are good boys, they sent back enough money for their sister's marriage, to build this house and buy 20 acres of land. Now my daughter and her husband have joined them. I am left alone in this huge house, so I brought my cousin's family to live with me."

Jagvinder Kaur's story is typical of the region that shows the social changes taking place in the countryside. But Gurinder Singh, a young doctor from Padhri Kalan village, about a day's ride from Amritsar, who migrated to Canada during the height of the militancy in Punjab provides another picture of the migratory traffic. Over the years, his parents and his siblings had joined him abroad, with the result that there was no one left in the village to farm the land. Finally, the doctor decided to leave his practice in Canada and go home. Returning to Padhri Kalan he went back to farming the land and got so involved in the village affairs that he was elected sarpanch of the village a few years later.

Emigration has become a widespread industry that is among the most visible in the Punjab countryside. Travel agents have sprouted in every corner of the state as also migration agents who claim to be able to arrange a visa to any country for a price. The migration business is now a corporate enterprise with an Association of Professional Immigration Consultancies in Punjab that includes all agencies registered with the government. The larger agencies have spread out beyond Punjab, taking their skills to other states in the country as the migration bug spreads to new areas. The migration rush has spawned a number of lucrative, ancillary business enterprises. English teaching institutes dot the countryside to prepare the prospective migrant for life abroad; many also run courses on how an applicant should conduct himself during the interview with the all-powerful visa officer. Studying abroad is the simplest way of getting the prized visa, and there are agencies that promise admission to a foreign university or institute to any student who can produce a school-leaving certificate. With the large number of NRIs coming back to marry, scores of finishing schools for girls have cropped up in the small towns that claim to prepare them to match the NRI needs.

As the diaspora enhances India's influence around the world, it has also begun increasing its influence in domestic politics. Diasporas have played an important role in facilitating international trade for they can provide channels for flow of information as well as the mechanisms for concluding contracts in the countries where they reside. They also help in entrepreneurial start-ups among the migrant community as they provide the necessary information, access and resources for new ventures. Diasporas help to create markets for home country goods and also enhance the reputation of home country products and services. The Indian diaspora's success in Silicon Valley helped to create a worldwide brand image for India's IT expertise in terms of quality and cost-effectiveness.

A good part of Indian exports are linked to the overseas community. The overseas market has become increasingly important for exporters of Indian films, music, arts, crafts, garments, wedding paraphernalia etc. The overseas Indian tastes and requirements have had an even more pervasive effect on Indian movies. Films are simultaneously released in India and the foreign market. They are no longer restricted to the ethnic markets. The combined sale of satellite rights, overseas rights and the DVD market have become a big chunk of the revenue from any major film. It is therefore natural that the beautiful foreign locales, the dancing and the costumes, and to some extent even the script and the songs are all tailored to appeal to the overseas Indian audience.

Films that incorporate themes familiar to overseas Indians or based in diasporic settings consciously target foreign viewers. Films like Monsoon Wedding and Bend It Like Beckham made by overseas Indians that were commercial hits on the foreign film circuit have helped break the barrier against Indian films in the western countries. The latest trend in the Mumbai film industry is to shoot two versions of a feature film – a long, Hindi version packed with song, dance and drama and a shorter version in English sans the songs for the international market.

Indian films were popular in many Third World countries because of their themes of social justice. But recent day Indian films no longer have a social message; they are vivid celebrations of urban wealth with music that is not entirely unfamiliar to a globalised audience. Films that become hits show elaborate weddings and festivals, family feuds, ornate havelis, picture postcard locations; underlying all this is a stereotypical storyline of a good joint family. It is the picture of exotic India that gets replicated in the high-grossing Indian films. According to film star and social activist, Shabana Azmi: "A synthetic sheen covers the whole of contemporary India and overseas Indians rejoice in a cinematic celebration of the wonder that is India."

The overseas Indian market has had its impact on the Indian art and culture scene as well. It has become an increasingly important factor in changing patterns of cultural performances. Like itinerant gurus and preachers, Indian musicians, vocalists and classical dancers undertake regular foreign tours that are financially more rewarding than performances at home. Sagarika Ghose wrote in the Indian Express of a well-known Bharatnatayam dancer who was repeatedly asked to portray "angst" and "alienation" through her dance. When told that Bharatnatayam is not about angst or alienation, the acclaimed dancer was informed that overseas Indian audiences would not sponsor her if she remained overtly traditional. So an ersatz tradition was being manufactured by the NRIs, wrote Ghose, created to suit personal imagined needs.

The overseas Indian community has become an important market for Indian art with the result that prices have skyrocketed. A Tyeb Mehta triptych fetched a record Rs 1.5 crore at an auction in 2003. But Indian art critics' hold that only a small group of well-known names in the Indian art scene command the new escalated prices. In the last decade prices for certain artists have climbed about a thousand times. They have become a glamorous brand name for wealthy overseas Indians to display on drawing room walls and corporate offices. A new breed of collectors has developed among the high earning middle level executive. This phenomenon has distorted valuations in the Indian art world creating a vast gulf in the prices of Indian art works. It is a bit like the gulf between the endorsements that cricket receives in comparison with other sporting events like hockey and football in India. The middle rung of artists or those artists whose work does not appeal to the nostalgic overseas Indian are unlikely to get similar recompense for their creative work.

NRIs have become important collectors of Indian contemporary art. The high prices in the overseas market means that some artists no longer innovate or experiment with new ideas.

The prosperous overseas Indian looks for something familiarly Indian that blends with popular western styles and techniques. Since the boom in Indian art began in the 1980s overseas Indians have purchased modernistic paintings of Hindu gods and goddesses and other popular Indian themes. The artists tend to repeat themselves to satisfy the high paying market. It makes the art works into another kind of trophy, a new acquisition that is a must buy for the wealthy NRI. Overseas market forces have dictated the trends in Indian art and not always to the benefit of Indian art, according to the critics.

In the literary world, VS Naipaul and Salman Rushdie are writers of Indian origin, who have had a far-reaching effect on Indian writing in English. Their provocative writings have evoked strong official reactions as well as stormy public debates in India. With Midnight's Children, Salman Rushdie broke away from convention, using a chutnified (Indianised) English and painted a picture of Indian reality in an Indianised language and style that caught the imagination. By breaking several stylistic and subject taboos of Indian writing, Rushdie's highly successful experiment with magic realism changed the way in which Indian writers wrote about India. It opened the way for Indian writers to unselfconsciously use Indianisms in their work.

The 1990s were an exciting period in Indian publishing with three best-selling authors, Rushdie, Vikram Seth and Arundhati Roy opening up the market for a new a wave of Indian writing in English by authors who used it as a first language. The international success of the new Indian novels opened the doors to a hybrid, diasporic cultural identity that celebrates the cultural mix of the migrant writer by entwining strands picked from the host society with the ethnic roots. Diasporic Indian writing is beginning to have its impact on writing in India as well, especially as Indian writers in English look for a larger foreign readership. The Indian Council of Cultural Affairs organised a conference on Indian

Writing in English at the Neemrana Resort in 2002, which brought together writers based in India and abroad. It had its stormy moments, but the passions aroused during the discussions were indicative of the fact that both categories were affected by each other's criticism and acclaim.

For long India has taken the diaspora for granted, as a community that would forever be linked to the homeland by bonds of Indian culture. In the communication age, urban India is being swept by the influence of those who live far away but retain a touch of Indianness. As diasporic groups the world over have gained wealth and recognition in their adopted countries, home governments are increasingly trying to use them to further their interests in the western capitals where they reside. Governments around the world find their diaspora in America useful to promote their interests in the United States. In turn, diasporas are becoming increasingly influential in their homelands. Their wealth and security, access to power centres in western capitals, to financial hubs and the modern electronic communication systems gives them the opportunity to play a significant role in homeland politics.

The Economist of June 4, 2003 related how the Chicago based Alexander the Great Foundation had mounted a campaign to have an image of Alexander carved out on a mountainside in northern Greece. Alexander the Great has acquired iconic status among the Greek diaspora and the giant sculpture was meant as a reminder that his empire covered northern Greece. Diasporic groups try to reproduce the styles and customs of their new homes and the Alexander effigy would be four times the size of effigies of American presidents carved out on the side of Mount Rushmore. Even though the Greek government was unenthusiastic about the project, it came under tremendous pressure from rich American Greeks. The giant statue project shows the diasporic need to glorify their history and historical figures to exult in their civilizational history in the new country.

Migrants have a feeling of being voiceless in the new society and many of them seek emotional sustenance by reinforcing their ties with the homeland. They try to stay in touch with local politics at home and use various means to connect with the homeland. One of the most vicarious methods of connection is to participate in the political processes and discourse of the homeland. Exiles and migrants have for long been a factor in their country's politics, whether in the struggle for freedom from an imperial power or a change of regime in the homeland.

The Internet has added another dimension to the connectivity with the homeland that has resulted in the phenomenon that the historian, Benedict Anderson has called 'long distance nationalism'. The Internet has enhanced the ability to stay in touch and increased the capacity of the diasporia to air their views on political matters in the homeland. It has also aided the formation of new networks of like-minded diasporic groups. The long distance nationalism that grips the migrant has an effect on the home country, which can range from the embarrassment of giant statues gifted by an over-enthusiastic diaspora to the damaging effect of their support to radical groups.

A large number of migrants remain on the fringes of local society in their new homes. Their sense of displacement and loneliness is assuaged to some extent by being involved in the political life of the mother country. However, the influence of their experiences in the new land changes their perspective with the result that their views and opinions need not necessarily follow the trends at home. Migration often results in a rephrasing of notions of national identity, and the migrants understanding of developments at home, so that their views can be completely at variance with the prevailing thought at home.

It is a small fraction of migrants who become politically active, but quite a few of those that do, adopt fairly reactionary and supra-nationalistic views. Whether it is the diasporic Irish or Serbs, Croats,

Albanians, West Africans, they have played destructive roles in times of strife and political turmoil at home. The American Irish raised money and supported Irish militant groups, including the Irish Republican Army. The international Tamil diaspora has served as fund collector for the Liberation Tigers of Tamil Eelam (LTTE). Support for the Tamil Tigers is projected as a patriotic duty among the Tamil diaspora and videos cassettes of LTTE battles are circulated to keep the patriotic fervour high and reduce support for the moderate Tamil groups. Tamils living in Europe and North America keep tabs on all news of interest and have a system of circulating articles of interest within the community. A critical reference results in a flurry of protests; from letter to editors, rejoinders, emails and at times even demonstrations to keep alive their point of view.

The growing influence of diasporic groups is becoming a subject of discussion for strategic analysts. A Rand Corporation report in 2003 held that ethnic diasporas had become a strategically important factor as an instrument of conflict with their capacity to get involved in the politics of their homeland. The report titled – The Security Dynamics of Demographic Factors by Brian Nichiporuk said that activist groups within ethnic diasporas can become a strategic asset that their home countries can draw upon to help them achieve regional politico-military objectives. Communication links and global banking nets increase the opportunities for globally distributed ethnic diasporas to play a key role in military campaigns involving their home state. The report warned that rival diasporas could engage themselves in violent conflict in their host countries in order to advance the causes of their respective home states. This can be done through extensive fundraising, an international public relations campaign to demonise opponents of the home state, or the extertion of pressure on governments in the host countries to turn against enemies of their home state, it said.

Long distance nationalism has had its destructive effect in India as well. The Sikhs in Canada, Britain and the US were easily swayed by the Khalistani appeal for a separate Sikh state, making them ready to donate time and money for the cause. Restoring the pristine quality of religious practice in the homeland strikes a deep chord among diasporic groups that takes them back to some fantasised historical memory.

Nostalgia and romanticised visions of the homeland make diasporic groups vulnerable to all kinds of demands on their sense of ethnic belonging. They become easy prey for the visiting fund collector. Fundamentalist or separatist movements in almost all the South Asian countries have looked for moral and material support from the overseas diasporic communities, whether they be the overseas Sikhs, the Sri Lankan Tamils or the Mirpuris living in Britain. The political parties are also not averse to tapping the overseas communities for support, like the Overseas Friends of BJP and its various offshoots and the Overseas Congress affiliates. Village factional politics of Punjab are quickly transmitted across the seas, to the overseas brethren who maintain a keen interest in local politics; Punjab politicians and Sikh leaders visit regularly to draw support and contributions from the overseas community.

The overseas Indian builds a vision of India that he has no intention of living in. He patronises, funds and supports causes like Khalistan or other more obscurantist movements. He has a skewed version of nationalism that has little to do with his own actions. It is a remembered form of culture without the creative strains that flow through in the homeland. He is the raucously patriotic NRI flying the tricolour at cricket matches and other sporting events. NRIs are wont to loudly proclaim their views on what is wrong with India; some of them believe that a spell of dictatorship would be the best solution for India's turbulent politics. The migrant's vision of India can be radically different from the vision of those who live in the old country, but the Internet allows the migrant to make his radical views a part of the public discourse.

The information highway has provided a new means of expression, giving the migrant a safe space to express his increasingly nationalistic and jingoistic views. It provides the means to give an instant reaction to events back home. The South Asian community with their IT skills have taken to the Internet as an important weapon for political communication and propaganda. Migrant groups can send off hundreds of emails disseminating their views around the world in a simple click of the mouse. Their prescriptions may not match the interests or aspirations of the people back home. They are often not aware or not willing to understand the implication of their demands, which provide a momentary glow of bravado. Email activism got a boost after the nuclear tests in South Asia in 1998 as overseas Indians and Pakistans gloried in the nuclear tests. There was a surge of pride in the glory of India's history, and anger at the betrayals of the past. Pop patriotism has a different resonance when the individual is far from home, one that draws on the feelings of guilt, for as Indians westernise they feel the need to display louder signs of nationalism.

Cyber nationalism can easily flow into the political discourse at home with dangerous consequences as the Internet can blur the distinction between the overseas Indian and the Indian at home. It can help to incite passions at home since Internet users can air the most rabid ideas on the net; for the anonymity of the Internet allows them to propound views that they would be reluctant to express except in closed circles of like-minded people. They cannot be held accountable for what they write on a bulletin board on the net, and they do not have to live with the consequences of their rabid nationalism and the policies that they advocate. The flow of cyber-hate in 2002 was at its peak when tensions between India and Pakistan were high and the two countries had mobilised their troops along the border. Overseas Indians were vociferously demanding that India declare war and drop nuclear bombs on Pakistan.

Diasporas can be a double-edged weapon, for they can develop their own agenda and become highly effective pressure groups on the home government. According to Prof Bhiku Parekh, Centennial Professor at the London School of Economics, long distance nationalism was always dangerous. Prof Parikh explained: "The politics of Israel has been gravely distorted by the politics of the Jewish diaspora. We in India suffered at the hands of the overseas support for Khalistan. It is therefore extremely important that while the government in India should evoke and mobilise the patriotism of the diaspora, it must also remember that the diaspora has its own agenda, has its own legitimate concern. And therefore on both sides the long distance patriotism must be handled with great care and sensitivity."

The diaspora has an increasing and far-reaching influence in India in the social, political, economic and commercial spheres. Faster travel and communication has led to a greater interaction between overseas Indians and the homeland. A comprehensive, balanced diaspora policy that engages the different sections of the overseas community can enhance the gains from the diaspora while keeping its negative aspects in check.

Chapter 14

Policy of Engagement

The Indian government has grappled with ways to address the expectations and grievances of the overseas Indians for several years. The National Democratic Alliance government constituted a High Level Committee on the diaspora and set up a division headed by an Additional Secretary in the Ministry of External Affairs. It organised an annual high profile *Pravasi Bharatiya Divas* and instituted the *Pravasi Awards*. The United Progressive Alliance government gave an added focus to diaspora matters by constituting a separate Ministry headed by a Minister of State (Independent charge). There is little doubt that interaction with the diaspora is multi-faceted and mutually advantageous, but to get the maximum benefit the government needs to devise a comprehensive, pragmatic policy taking into account the interests of the different segments of the overseas community.

India has a highly diversified diaspora and its policy must include elements catering to each section, and should seek to develop a common identity within the diaspora as a whole. At the same time, it is important that the government obtain acceptance and approval of the policy within the country. A diasporic identity can be cultivated only when overseas Indians feel welcomed in the homeland.

The perceived pampering of overseas Indians from America and Britain has also increased the ambivalence in the attitude of ordinary Indians towards the overseas Indians. Most Indians have mixed feelings about NRIs as a group and they are unfavourably compared to the overseas Chinese who have fuelled the foreign direct investment in China. The bludgeoning NRI portfolio investments are dismissed as the result of purely monetary considerations and not due to any high sounding nationalistic sentiment.

This attitude has had its impact even on genuine investments by overseas Indians. State governments have offered special facilities to attract investment and overseas Indians have set up modern hospitals and medical centres in Andhra Pradesh and Tamil Nadu. Local residents have disparaged even these investments because the land was made available at concessional rates with an assured supply of water and electricity.

Indian government efforts to attract foreign investment has encouraged the overseas Indians in the US and Britain to make their own demands on what they expect from India, from greater financial concessions to dual citizenship to seats in the Rajya Sabha. The excessive attention lavished on rich overseas Indians leads them to believe that India needs them, their skills and their guidance. The media celebration of the migrant achievements and the official pampering of overseas Indians gives them an exaggerated sense of importance that has a sharply negative impact on the image of NRIs in India. Deep down middle class Indians resent the slavish attention and the NRI tendency to give patronising, ill-informed advice. Many migrants feel that they have an added right to give advice to the folks at home when they are making a contribution to the economy.

Columnist Pritish Nandy once wrote in a scathing article in *The Hindustan Times* of January 20, 2003, saying that the government and the media had anointed the NRIs as the heroes of modern India. Glowing reports appeared in the media about their success stories, with dazzling stories about their wealth and influence, the deeply conservative life they live, the traditional values that they cherish, the donations they make to build temples out there and colleges here. For years, NRIs have supported groups in the Sangh parivar as well as the Congress – in the hope of influencing government policy. "All we get from our NRIs is gratituitous advice and boastful success stories that we can easily do without. They need India. India does not need them. They need the emotional anchoring this great country offers – even as they make their millions elsewhere."

These are sentiments that exist, in milder or even more strident terms, within the country. India and the overseas Indians cannot have a mutually satisfactory relationship while such sentiments linger in the Indian mind. The impression that the government is pampering the overseas community without adequate returns is quite damaging to the prospects of a fruitful relationship. On the other hand, Indian migrants feel that the government is only paying attention to them for their money.

There is clearly a greater need for the government to explain its diaspora policy to both overseas Indians and its own citizens at home. Overseas Indians will invest time, money and sentiment in India only if their efforts are appreciated and acknowledged by not just in some government circles but also by the people. That acknowledgement will not be forthcoming if the feeling persists that NRIs are being treated as favoured "sons-in-law". The government needs to bridge the divide between the new and the old diaspora in order to create a common diasporic feeling, for the strength of its soft power through its overseas community is enhanced by the diaspora's size and spread across the world.

The relationship can be productive only if India is seen to benefit from the relationship and the diaspora values its ties with India. India is not the only country to have offered special incentives and facilities to its diaspora. Other countries like Greece, Turkey, Spain, China, Lebanon, Egypt, Thailand, Pakistan, Sri Lanka are also devising cultural and social means by which the links to the mother country can be kept alive.

Need for Engagement

India's overseas community is among the largest diasporas in the world. Spread over more than 100 countries, it gives India a worldwide presence that makes it a significant facet of India's foreign policy. The diaspora acts as an important asset and its presence has deep implications in India's bilateral relations with many countries. Indian communities are politically influential in a number of countries. There are more that 250 Members of Parliament of Indian origin in legislatures around the world, and many more of part Indian descent like Sebastian Edathy, the Co-chairman of the Indo-German Parliamentary Forum.

The Indian community in the US has actively lobbied for Indian interests in the US Congress at the time of the nuclear related economic sanctions and the Kargil conflict. The international reaction to India's nuclear tests in 1998 brought forth a large number of influential overseas Indians who acted as pressure groups to put across the Indian position to their governments in capitals around the world from London, Washington, Berlin and Johannesburg.

India has often used the goodwill of the overseas Indians to obtain access in different ways. As consumers of Indian goods, overseas Indians have provided a market for Indian exports; they have also helped Indian companies to establish themselves in the countries where they are settled. Overseas Indians have helped to project Indian interests in western capitals. They have access to the power centres and financial centres in their countries. Indians hold influential positions in politics, business, social and economic life of the countries where they are settled. They are leading academics, authorities in their fields of specialisation, business tycoons, top scientists and innovators and celebrities of various kinds. Their success in the IT sector has enhanced India's image worldwide as a knowledge country.

The Indian government looks for foreign direct investment and remittances for portfolio management from overseas Indians, it seeks the overseas community's support to further India's interests in the countries where they are settled. It wants to strengthen its cultural links with Indians around the world.

The diaspora wants to remain linked with India, with its culture, value systems and religious traditions. Overseas Indians want to connect their children to India, the ancestral land from which they draw their ethnic identity. For the majority of the old diaspora in countries like Mauritius, Fiji, Suriname and South Africa, it is cultural sustenance that they look for from India. Governments in countries like Trinidad and Suriname have sought better connectivity with India, through regular flights and direct shipping to India. Overseas Indian organisations have asked for visa free entry to India, education facilities in India and more student exchange programmes to stimulate their interest in India and its culture. They want cultural centres to be set up for regular cultural interaction.

The Indian population in almost every country has sought educational facilities in India; in recent years Indians in the US have looked for seats in Indian medical colleges because of the prohibitive cost of medical education in America. They have proposed setting up of a special department in existing medical colleges for overseas students. Leaders in Mauritius suggested to the High Level Committee that the Indian government set up a separate university for PIOs in India for children of the diaspora. They have asked for courses teaching Ayurveda and other Indian systems of medicine.

The new migrants in the US and Britain, who have close ties with the homeland, have a higher level of demands from the Indian government. They had demanded dual citizenship and are now seeking nominated seats in Parliament. These overseas Indians want greater safety and security of their investments in India and assistance in getting repossession of their property from tenants and encroachers. They have asked for contact cells in the central and state governments for fast track disposal of problems relating to overseas Indians. Some PIO associations have sought special facilities and incentives to invest in entrepreneural ventures in India and asked for a single point clearance system for new ventures. PIOs, who want to contribute to public works in their home areas, have complained about the rigidity of bureaucratic systems in the implementation of philanthropic projects.

Means of Engaging Each Other

The basic feature of India's diaspora policy should be focused on infusing a common diasporic identity with the overseas community and linking the emotional and cultural ties with India. The quest for investment and influence should flow from that basic thrust of the diaspora policy. Education, learning Indian languages, dance, music, arts and crafts, visiting the ancestral homeland, India TV programmes are some of the ways of keeping intact the cultural ties. Some of the ways of keeping connected with the diaspora could even become viable commercial enterprises.

Education

Education is an area of vital interest for the diaspora, for its success is intrinsically linked to education, as it has been the primary means for economic advancement. A large number of Indians go abroad to study, many of whom may be the next generation of overseas Indians. Australia runs an aggressive marketing campaign around the world, emphasising its competitive cost of education and easier visa regulations to attract foreign students. Education is now listed as Australia's third largest service export industry and constitutes a $ 4 billion industry that provides employment as well as revenue for Australia's economy and helps funding higher education in the country.

Australia granted 162,575 student visas in the year 2002-2003. The Australian overseas student programme is meant to "increase understanding of other cultures, build friendships and future networks for Australian students and promote Australia's reputation as a knowledge country in the international community." The Australian programme is regulated under its Overseas Students Act of 2000 and run by the Education Service for Overseas Students (ESOC).

Like Australia, India can also enter the field of education for overseas students to offer cost-effective higher education for foreign students and overseas Indians at a market determined fee structure. Education is an important tool for moulding of minds and building emotional and intellectual connections. It can be both an economic activity as well as fulfil the diaspora's need for education. India used to be a favoured destination for students from developing countries when several thousand African and Malaysian foreign students used to study in Indian universities and professional colleges in the 1960s and 70s. India can regain its reputation as a centre of learning by opening out the education sector for foreign students.

Education is a highly regulated sector in India with a strong ideological underpinning. Regarded as a public duty, higher education is highly subsidised. But educational facilities for foreign students can be opened through creating new colleges so as not to burden the state run institutions. India has a global brand in the Indian Institutes of Technology (IIT) and Indian Institute of Management (IIM) and can build on that brand as a provider of quality education. IIMs have been requested by several foreign governments to either open a branch in their countries or prepare a module for them. Private Indian institutions such as Manipal University already have their branches in Nepal and Malaysia.

With the experience of the industry supported Indian School of Business in Hyderabad, government can allow private enterprise in setting up similar self-financing educational institutions for Indian and foreign students. Private boarding schools have already come up around the country for the children of Indians living abroad, offering educational and residential facilities to match the expectations of their parents.

The government can constitute an overseas educational council to oversee education for overseas students. Some of the new private engineering and medical colleges approved by the state governments could be allowed to upgrade with better facilities to accept foreign students and charge appropriate fees. With the growing willingness to combine some aspects of alternative medicine and traditional herbal therapies with modern health care, courses on the Indian systems of medicine can be taught at the medical colleges.

The corporate hospitals and super-speciality medical centres already cater to patients from the Gulf countries and Britain where the National Health Service places non-emergency surgery at the bottom of a long waiting list. State governments have provided infrastructural facilities like land, water and roads for corporate hospitals on the condition that they treat a set number of poor patients. Due to poor implementation of the programme, the projects have not always worked satisfactorily, but with tighter scrutiny it is a pattern that can be replicated in collaboration with overseas Indian doctors.

Teaching Indian Languages

Indians in countries like Mauritius, Trinidad and Tobago, Suriname and America look for teaching material and educational aids for teaching Indian languages. According to UNDP's *Human Development Report (2004)* the Chinese diaspora safeguards the survival of its languages by importing books, supporting cultural associations and sending students to Chinese universities. In addition, there are Chinese language schools where the Chinese community can study in Chinese as the medium of instruction. Promotion of Chinese language has been the method used by China to hold on to the loyalty of its diaspora.

Language is one of the most important means to carry over the cultural values and traditions to the younger generation. But it has usually been the case that language skills fade away by the third generation of migrants. The second generation are bilingual, but their children often retain only a smattering of words from the ancestral language, unless they live within their own ethnic community. In Trinidad the urban Indians slowly lost knowledge of the language spoken by their grandparents, but the popularity of Indian films and music has revived an interest in the language. Small Indian communities have kept alive their traditional languages with a great deal of effort, through informal and home teaching and Sunday afternoon classes in temples.

The younger generation may learn to speak their mother tongue, but there are few books available to stimulate their interest in reading. Some Indian publishers produce children's books and Indian novels for the export market, but they are on the main part low cost publishing, shabbily printed in garish colours on low grade paper. There is a good market within the diaspora for well-produced, attractive books on Indian themes, but Indian publishers are reluctant to enter the field, as it is an unfamiliar market. Countries that have a large Indian population have occasionally asked for books on Indian themes. The government can support the production of well produced, low cost translations of epics, traditional literature and as well as contemporary literary works specially for the diasporic market.

The Indian Council for Cultural Relations (ICCR) is the government body that showcases Indian culture in other countries, but its activities are not geared to the diaspora. It sends Indian artistes and cultural troupes to tour foreign countries and invites foreign artistes to India. It also prepares material for dissemination abroad. But the diaspora has specific needs for maintaining the connection with Indian art and culture. The ICCR runs Indian Cultural Centres in countries with a large diasporic population, but it needs to facilitate the learning of Indian languages. It can support small centres to teach Indian languages that can be run by local cultural groups and the language classes can be conducted by local residents with the help of teaching aids and the material provided by the Indian government.

Government or other autonomous bodies can prepare quality teaching materials that are tailored for local communities or for individual learning. Further learning material in the form of CDs, audio and videocassettes that can be supplemented through interactive courses on the Internet. Interactive websites, films and video cassettes on different aspects of India, its culture, history, law and politics, and other distance learning programmes can spark off an interest in any age group to learn about one's culture. Attractively illustrated books in simple language for children as well as animated CDs and video-cassettes of Indian short stories and folk tales.

Media and Entertainment

Indian films have a wide audience appeal in many countries, even among people who do not understand the language. Indian film stars are recognized and feted in countries as diverse as the Central Asian republics, Mongolia, China, Turkey, Egypt and in Africa. For the fourth and fifth generation of Indian descent, there is a connection with India only through Indian films. Television has the potential to act as an opinion maker. Real time global television has already demonstrated its impact on foreign policy as it can often set the agenda with its instantaneous coverage of developing events. BBC World gives the British worldview while Al Jazeera has provided a voice to Arab public opinion. In the US, some foreign channels are directly beamed to providers and then distributed to home TVs. Some local entrepreneurs repackage programmes from satellite feeds or videotapes for their ethnic audiences.

Doordarshan DD has tried to market its programmes abroad but has failed to make much headway. However, it did have a short-term arrangement with Mauritius television with a nominal payment to telecast seven hours of its programmes in Mauritius. It had a very good feedback on that arrangement. Instead of trying unsuccessfully to earn revenue by selling its programmes, Doordarshan should enter into similar arrangement to reach a wider audience around the world. To begin with, it can provide a limited range of programmes to television channels and public broadcasting channels in countries with a substantial diaspora. In 2002 DD identified six languages apart from Hindi and English; Tamil, Telugu, Bengali, Malayalam, Punjabi and Gujarati that had an audience abroad. Overseas Indians want to know about developments in India, they want their children to watch some entertainment programmes in their mother tongue, and travel and cultural programmes.

Under the Tenth Five Year Plan Doordarshan and All India Radio were allocated Rs. 100 crores to make a series of programmes on Indian classics in all Indian languages. The series directed by noted filmmaker Gulzar on Munshi Premchand's works for Doordarshan, has a wide-ranging appeal. Such programmes build another bridge between overseas Indians and their Indian heritage. The *Ramayana* and *Mahabharat* TV serials, social dramas and film based programmes are perennial favourites among overseas Indian audiences.

Tourism

As the Indian tourist industry tries to position India as an exciting tourist destination with the '*Incredible India*' campaign, the diaspora is a huge segment that can be tapped in a systematic way. Innovative packages with some special attractions are the means used worldwide to draw the tourist. People of Indian origin form about 28 per cent of all tourist arrivals in India, many of whom come to India to visit relatives. But India can be projected as a fun, exotic tourist location for a holiday with a difference for young people of Indian origin, while pilgrimage packages and tours of cultural heritage sites would appeal to the older generation.

The Gujarat state government marketed the *Navratri* celebrations in 2003 as a tourist attraction for the foreign visitor. Though it was not successful in bringing in foreign tourists, the campaign attracted the non-resident Gujaratis to time their trip home for the festival days. *Garba* dancing, traditional crafts and festival food charmed the high spending visitors. Gujarat tourism now plans to make the festival package an annual event. A young entrepreneur in Rajasthan is advertising his renovated *haveli* (spacious house) as a venue for a memorable, traditional Indian wedding.

Boodhun Teelock of Mauritius had to hire the services of a detective to locate his ancestral village but the Uttar Pradesh State Tourism Department has since launched its *Discover Your Roots* programme that helps people trace their ancestral connections in the state. UP Tourism's website offers to locate places that have links to the ancestors of overseas Indians or people who served in India during the colonial period. Old passports, land records, letters, school certificates and even old clothes with local tailors' tags have provided the clues to discover old connections. Guyana's President Bharrat Jagdeo was given a rousing welcome when he visited his ancestral village. He had an emotional meeting with an old grandaunt, who recalled that she had heard about her husband's cousin who had gone across the seas some years before her marriage.

Philanthropy

The general impression in India is that overseas Indians do little for India, but overseas Indians have contributed handsomely during natural disasters and war, from 1962, through 1965 and 1971. The real spurt in overseas donations came in 2001 after the Gujarat earthquake, when there was an outpouring of relief material and medical teams from the overseas community.

The United States has a strong tradition of philanthropy; its elite institutions and colleges are endowed with huge bequests. The high public role of philanthropy in the West has moved Indians into making their own contributions to charitable purposes, initially for building temples in the US and Britain. They have made donations to religious organisations for charitable work in India, and many of them send money to their relatives to spend on charity or on specific projects. Contributions have increased in the recent years because many American companies have a system of making matching contributions to the money donated by their employees to specified organisations.

Overseas Indians experience with philanthropy in India is a chequered one since the government does not have a coherent policy on how charitable bequests from the diaspora is to be treated. Many have unpleasant experiences to relate about their dealings with the local bureaucracy in their home districts when they have tried to set up schools, health centres, temples in their home villages. Many have been frustrated with their attempts to get clearances and approvals for their projects while some have faced hostility from the district officialdom and local leaders who see them as rich outsiders to be fleeced. Others have returned after a few years of a project being completed to find that village politics and factionalism have overtaken the project.

To cite another Chinese example, provincial and city authorities actively woo overseas Chinese to contribute to special programmes in the homeland. They maintain lists of overseas Chinese from their regions who can be tapped for different kinds of support, from cash contributions to help in kind. Overseas Chinese are invited by the authorities to visit the projects when they are completed to build on their emotional ties and sense of achievement. The China Foundation was started in 1997 as a non-profit, charitable organisation for raising funds to improve basic health services and elementary education projects in underdeveloped rural areas in China.

Alumni contributions to the IITs dried up after Murli Manohar Joshi as Human Resource Development Minister publicly objected to alumni donations for a hostel for IIT Powai as luxurious and wasteful. The ministry issued a government order that all contributions to government run educational institutions had to be made to a new central fund called the *Bharat Shiksha Kosh* (Indian Education Fund). By the time the fund was scrapped 18 months later by the new government, the *Bharat Shiksha Kosh* had received less than Rs. 2000. Americans get tax rebates on donations to the alma mater, but not for contributions to overseas funds.

The controversy over the *Bharat Shiksha Kosh* directive sent an intensely negative signal about the government's attitude towards philanthropic contributions. Overseas Indians have a natural suspicion of the government machinery and would rather send their contributions to non-governmental organisations or religious organisations with a well-known reputation for charitable work. Contributors usually want a say in how their money is utilised; they want a sense of satisfaction at their donation being well spent. but sometimes their suggestions can become a point of dispute between the donors and the recipients. These are not intractable problems.

The government can constitute a high level, autonomous body with representatives of reputed NGOs to advise prospective donors on how to canalise their donations, on projects that require financial assistance in the areas they are interested in. It would bring a measure of transparency in the utilisation of philanthropic donations. The organisation could keep track of the utilisation of the funds and send a periodic report to the donors. Many overseas Indians have time and skills to offer for short periods such as during their annual vacations in India. They could contribute by holding seminar, lectures or training modules on a variety of subjects. Such an institution can prepare the database to match the skills on offer with the organisations that can benefit from their expertise. It could act as a centre for clearing the arrangements on both sides.

Investment and Remittances

The government's dependency on mobilising foreign exchange bank deposits from NRIs is now a thing of the past. During the years of foreign exchange shortages, the government had initiated several attractive deposit schemes to entice NRIs to invest their savings in Indian banks. These schemes have, however, been a fairly expensive method of resource mobilisation because of the very high rates of interest offered. The NRI deposits had become over 25 per cent of the country's total external debt. With the foreign exchange reserves in a healthy position, the Reserve Bank of India has progressively lowered the interest rates during 2003-04 and the Finance Minister has proposed to withdraw the tax waiver on the interest income in his budget speech. The NRI term deposits have proved to be volatile because of the short notice required for withdrawal. This volatility has been one of the reasons why Indians believe that overseas Indians are fair weather depositors, giving the example of the flight of NRI capital that led to the balance of payments crisis in 1991.

Foreign investment in India is directly related to the government policies for different sectors and the facilities and procedures for setting up the project. Other countries offer special incentives to make themselves an attractive destination for foreign investment. The government can expect overseas Indians to make investments when adequate returns can be expected and the facilities available match those in other regions of the world. In both cases, it is the ambivalent government policy, with ad hoc and often arbitrary decisions coupled with systemic and procedural delays that have put off the prospective investors and contributors.

The government should support the setting up of an Overseas Indian Foundation comprising mainly of overseas Indians with a few prominent Indian members for an interface between the global Indian family. The strength of the diaspora lies in its size, but the different segments of the diaspora need to be knitted into a common identity as an Indian diaspora. The Foundation could hold meetings in different countries to involve a large number of people of Indian origin and generate fellow feeling among the diaspora as a whole. It could provide the means for networking amongst the diaspora for business opportunities as well as transfer of skills and technology. The Indus Entrepreneurs or TIE was set up by rich Silicon Valley entrepreneurs to give help and guidance to young South Asians to start up their own ventures at a time when the well-networked Chinese professionals were being funded by relatives in Hong Kong and Taiwan. TIE's success led to Indians in Trinidad and Fiji asked for a TIE chapter to be set up in their countries. Linkages within the Indian communities worldwide will open up opportunities for the diaspora as a whole. The Foundation can be the organising group to bring overseas Indians together in different places.

Through a century and a half the diaspora has kept alive its cultural identity, despite being cut off from the ancestral land. But all sections of overseas Indians worry about the effects of modern day lifestyles and western influences through education and mass media that are increasingly affecting their children. Keeping alive the cultural connections will help in building the bridges between the different segments of the diaspora.

Chapter 15

Maintaining the Bonds Conclusion

Diasporas around the world have gained increasing prominence in recent decades. The second half of the 20th century, since the post-world war years has been a period of almost continuous migration to Europe and North America. Large-scale international migrations to the more developed economies have created transnational communities linked to different regions of the world. Better communications and cheaper transportation have increased the visibility and impact of diasporic groups within the international system. Countries with large migrant populations are also beginning to acknowledge the pluralistic character of their societies and .are actively pursuing policies to integrate the migrants into the local societies.

International migration has acquired a place in the public agendas of many countries because of growing concerns about its capacity to influence economic, political and social issues in the host countries. Globalisation of trade and easier capital flows has made it increasingly difficult to stop the global movement of people for the process of economic globalisation influences international migratory patterns. One effect of globalisation has been to facilitate the movement of capital, goods, services, labour, knowledge, and ideas across borders. Economic globalisation increases the volume of migrants and the 1990s saw a significant increase in the international mobility of highly skilled workers.

As the developed economies create new jobs, young people from developing countries migrate to fill the jobs, especially if they are jobs that the local people are unwilling to do. Migrants take up jobs at, both the upper and the lower end of the job market. The market for the technically skilled migrant is competitive as affluent countries seek to attract well-qualified professionals. When Germany opened up its IT sector for foreign software engineers three years ago, it could find applicants for barely a third of the jobs on offer because prospective Indian migrants found salaries in the United States much more attractive.

According to the United Nations Population Report, international migration will remain high during the next few decades. Demographic trends show that most of the developed countries will experience a population decline because of low birth rates and aging populations. On the other hand, the population in developing countries is much younger and population growth levels are higher. The larger aging population in rich countries will mean that they will require migrant workers to do the work that the local population is unable or unwilling to do. The opening of the services sector that is currently under negotiation at the WTO would also give a fillip to the cross border movement of workers for varying lengths of time. The services sector is the fastest growing sector in the world economy. International migrations are likely to continue in the coming decades in all categories of migrants, from temporary migrants, to seasonal and agricultural labour to highly skilled corporate expatriates.

The Indian diaspora can be expected to increase in size in the next couple of decades in line with the international trends of migration. The number of second generation Indians in the United

States, Britain, Australia and Canada will increase, as the majority of overseas Indians in these countries are relatively young. India has a young population and migration will be a likely avenue providing attractive work opportunities for India's educated youth, especially as a large number of young Indians are going abroad to study. Indians constitute the largest group of foreign students in the United States. The American embassy in Delhi estimates that there were about 75,000 Indians students in the US in 2002-03, an increase of 12 per cent from the previous year. Countries like Britain and Australia have a regular campaign to attract students from India. Many among the large number of Indians studying in foreign universities will join the ranks of immigrants and expatriates and look for jobs abroad.

In the past couple of decades, the overseas community has grown into an energetic and confident diaspora over 20 million strong that has given India a presence in many parts of the world. A successful, prosperous and politically influential diaspora is an asset to India, for it acts as a vibrant bridge between two countries, adding sustenance to their bilateral relations. It is not a one-way interaction that benefits only one side; both India and the diaspora have something to gain from the connection, in real as well as intangible terms.

Maintaining the bonds between India and the people of Indian origin is an emotional need for overseas Indians; it has economic advantages for India and helps in good bilateral relations between India and the country where the overseas Indians are domiciled. The influence of the politically active Indians in America was in evidence at the time of India's international isolation after the nuclear tests in 1998 and during the Kargil conflict in 1999.

The diaspora's interactions with India are likely to increase as the new migrants remain in closer touch with the homeland and often return home after some years abroad. Easier connectivity has made it easier to travel more frequently for migrants and their families. The growth in the Indian economy has also led to a more mobile diaspora, with overseas Indians returning home to work for short periods.

While comparing the Indian diaspora with the Chinese one, it would be well to recall that China has shown a remarkable consistency in their hospitable and welcoming attitude towards the diaspora, including returned overseas Chinese. China's FDI driven growth is backed by a range of incentives and facilities that have helped the prospective investor to make use of the low manufacturing costs in the country. The real advantage for the overseas Chinese was that they spoke the language, were familiar with the cultural milieu and could understand how the system worked. The Chinese government held job fairs in Silicon Valley to lure back overseas Chinese to start or be part of high-tech companies in Shanghai's newly developed Pudong district. Indians and Chinese started almost 30 per cent of the new start-ups in Silicon Valley. And if provided a similar investment environment like the overseas Chinese were offered, more Indian migrants would be willing to invest in business enterprises in the homeland.

Remittances from emigrants have become an important segment of the economy of several developing countries, forming a significant part of the GDP and the major part of the capital inflow into the country. Remittances are an important inflow of capital into the rural economy in several Indian states. Migration has opened up a veritable cottage industry for migration, with private recruiting agencies, travel agencies, migration assistance outfits, overseas education facilitation companies and their ancillary enterprises to prepare students for studying abroad, that have opened up in the countryside.

The diaspora policy needs to be tailored to the interests of the different groups of the diaspora. The post-World War emigrants who have done well in the developed countries are more forceful in articulating their expectations from the Indian government, but the needs of the older diaspora also require a similar level of attention in India. It is the size and spread of the overseas community that gives it an added importance. The presence of people of Indian descent in almost every corner of the world increases the reach of India's soft power. As Indians bring skills and technology to different parts of the world they enhance the global awareness of India as a modern nation. Overseas Indians need to build up networks amongst themselves connecting the people of Indian origin from around the world. A diaspora well connected within itself will make the overseas community a more influential and potent group with a wider sphere of activity.

The Pravasi Divas honours the overseas Indians and gives them an opportunity to interact with the Indian government. At the same time, a greater awareness among Indians of the diaspora as an asset to India will reduce the negative feelings that still exist at the popular level in India. A separate Ministry for Overseas Indians Affairs was set up in May 2004 for a better-coordinated view of the diaspora and its different facets. For several years the official government focus has tended to concentrate on the diaspora's implications on foreign policy and investment issues. Its focus can be expanded to the areas of education, culture, tourism, labour, media and entertainment.

India and its diaspora can enrich each other in a spirit of mutual interest. The Indian diaspora is like a mass of variegated strands with differing forms and textures, each with its own needs and expectations. As, Satyam Joshi, a delegate to the Pravasi Divas from Alberta, Canada said: "Indianness is our heritage, we take pride in it and we want to sustain it. We see the networking and support among the other diasporas and want to develop on similar lines, to help each other and preserve our cultural links with the ancestral homeland." It is in this spirit that the overseas community wants to engage with India, and it is this spirit that should form the basis of India's engagement with its diaspora.

Select Bibliography

1. Ali, Ahmed, *Plantation to Politics,* Suva, University of the South Pacific, 1980.
2. Alexander, Garth, *Silent Invasion: The Chinese in Southeast Asia*, Macdonald, 1973.
3. Aurora, G.S., *The New Frontiersmen: A Sociological Study of Indian Immigrants in the United Kingdom*, Popular Prakashan, 1967.
4. Bacon, Jean, *Life Lines – Community, Family and Assimilation Among Asian Indian Immigrants,* Oxford University Press, 1996.
5. Bahri, Deepika, Vasudev, Mary, *Between the Lines: South Asians & Postcoloniality,* Philadelphia, Templeton University Press, 1996.
6. Barrier, Gerald N., (ed) *The Sikh Daispora: Migration and the Experience Beyond Punjab,* Chanakya Publications.
7. Brawley, Sean, *The White Peril: Foreign Relations aned Asian Immigration to Australasia & North America 1919-1978*, University of NSW Press, 1995.
8. Bissoondoyal, B., *The Truth about Mauritius*, Bharatiya Vidya Bhawan, 1987.
9. Carrington, Selwyn H.H., *The Sugar Industry and the Abolition of the Slave Trade (1775-1810)* University Press of Florida
10. Chan, Sucheng, *Asian Americans: An Interpretive History*, Twayne Publishers.
11. Chang, Gordon H., *Asian Americans and Politics – Perspectives, Experiences, Prospects,* Stanford University Press, 2001.
12. Chattopadhyaya, Harprasad, *Indians in Sri Lanka: A Historical Study,* OPS Publishers.
13. Dubey, Ajay, *Indian Diaspora: Global Identity*, Kalinga Publications, 2003.
14. Gosling, Peter L.A., Lim, Y.C., *Identity, Culture and Politics*, Maruzen, Asia.
15. Gunalitteke, Gordon, (ed) *Migration of Asian Workers to the Arab World,* United Nations University Press, 1986.

16. Gupta, Anirudh, *Indians Abroad; Asia and Africa*, Orient Longman, 1971.
17. Harris, Nigel, *Thinking the Unthinkable: The Immigration Myth Exposed*, IB Tauris Publishers, 2002.
18. Hazareesingh, K., *A History of Indians in Mauritius*, General Printing and Stationary Cy Ltd., 1950.
19. Helweg, Arthur Wesley, *Sikhs in England*, Oxford University Press, 1986.
20. Henning, C.G., *The Indentured Indian in Natal (1860-1917)*, Promilla & Co Publishers.
21. Jha, Uma Shankar, *South Africa – Retrospect & Prospect*, Jawahar Publications.
22. Judge, Paramjit S., *Punjabis in Canada: A Study of Formation of an Ethnic Community*, Chanakya Publications.
23. Kelly, John D., *A Politics of Virtue: Hinduism, Sexuality & Countercolonial Discourse in Fiji*, University of Chicago Press, 1991.
24. Kirkman, W.P., *Unscrambling an Empire: A Critique of British Colonial Policy 1956-66*, Chatto & Windus.
25. Kurien, George, Srivastava, Ram P., *Overseas Indians: A Study in Adaption*, Vikas Publishing, 1983.
26. Lal, Brij V., *Girmitiya: The Origins of Fiji Indians*, Journal of Pacific History, 1983.
27. Lepervanche, Marie M. de, *Indians in White Australia*, George Allen & Unwin, 1984.
28. Lim, Y.C., Gosling, Peter L.A., *The Chinese in Southeast Asia: Ethnicity and Economic Activity*, Maruzen, Singapore.
29. Mahajani, Usha, *The Role of Indian Minorities in Burma and Malaya*, Vora & Co, 1960
30. Marett, Valerie, *Immigrants Settling in the City*, Leicester University Press, 1989.
31. McPherson, Kenneth, *The Indian Ocean: A History of People and The Sea*, Oxford University Press, 1993.
32. Meer, Y.S., *Documents of Indentured Labour: Natal 1851-1917*, Unity Publications, 1980.
33. Melady, Thomas, Melady, Margaret, *Uganda: The Asian Exiles*, Cosmo Publications, 1976.
34. Millette, James, Society and Politics in Colonial Trinidad, Zed Books, 1985.
35. Moraes, Frank, *The Importance of Being Black*, Macmillian Company, 1965.
36. Morris, H.S., *Indians in Uganda*, Weidenfeld & Nicolson, 1968.
37. Nazareth, J.M., *Brown Man, Black Country*, Tidings Publications, 1981.
38. Pan, Lynn, *Sons of the Yellow Emperor, The Story of the Overseas Chinese*, London, Secker & Warburg.

39. Purcell, Victor, *The Chinese in Southeast Asia*, Oxford University Press, 1965.
40. Ram, Sodhi, *Indian Immigrants in Great Britain*, Inter-India Publications.
41. Robinson, Vaughan, *Transients, Settlers, and Refugees: Asians in Britain,* Clarendon Press, 1986.
42. Rodney, Walter, *A History of the Guyanese Working People 1945-1983,* Heinemann Educational Books.
43. Sahadevan, P., *India and Overseas Indians: The Case of Sri Lanka*, Kalinga Publications
44. Sanadhaya, Totaram, *My Twentyone Years in the Fiji Islands*, Fiji Museum, Suva, 1991.
45. Sandhu, K.S., Mani, A., (ed.) *Indian Communities in South East Asia*, Times Academic Press.
46. Sardesai, D.R., *Southeast Asia, Past and Present,* Vikas Publishing House.
47. Singh, Bhagat, *Canadian Society and Culture*, Vikas Publishing, 1997.
48. Singh, Bhagwan, Das, Parimal Kumar, *Fiji: The Changing Face*, Har-Anand Publications, 1995.
49. Singh, I.J. Bahadur, (ed) *Indians in the Caribbean,* Sterling Publishers.
50. Singh, Shubha, *Fiji: A Precarious Coalition*, Har-Anand Publications, 2001.
51. Spinner, Thomas J., *A Political and Social History of Guyana 1945-1983,* Westview Press.
52. Steel, David, *No Entry: The Background & Implications of the Commonwealth Immigrants Act, 1968,* London, C Hurst & Co, 1969.
53. Thapan, Anita Raina, *Sindhi Diaspora*, Ateno de Manila University Press.
54. Tinker, Hugh, *A New System of Slavery*, Oxford University Press, 1974.
55. Tinker, Hugh, *The Banyan Tree: Overseas Emigrants from India, Pakistan and Bangladesh,* Oxford University Press, 1977.
56. Verteuil, Anthony de, *Eight East Indian Immigrants,* Port of Spain, Paria Publishing Co., 1989.
57. Verma, Archana B., *The Making of Little Punjab in Canada*, Sage Publications, 2002.
58. Wiebe, Paul D, Mariappen, S., *Indian Malaysians: The View from the Plantation*, Manohar, 1978.
59. William Lea E., *The Future of Overseas Chinese in Southeast Asia*, McGraw Hill, 1966.
60. Wood, Donald, *Trinidad in Transition: The Years After Slavery*, Oxford University Press.

Index

Doordarshan 203